THE PRITIKIN®
PRINCIPLE

the calorie density solution

by Robert Pritikin

TIME
LIFE
BOOKS

Alexandria, Virginia

To my father, Nathan Pritikin, who pointed the way.

ACKNOWLEDGMENTS

First and foremost, Tom Monte deserves a medal for putting up with me and taking my stream of consciousness and turning it into a fine piece of writing. My father introduced me to Tom and told me that if he was ever to write a story of his life, Tom was to be that writer. He was and still is "our" writer.

Dr. Jay Kenney inspired this book—he introduced me to the calorie density research concept and has been a mentor and critic all along.

But the huge effort of our Nutrition staff really made this book the practical guide it had to be. Rebecca Fraley, R.D., put together the Calorie Density Index and with Maria McIntosh, R.D., did the menu planning, and with Kelly Gascoigne did the Dining Out section (and she lost 10 pounds in the process!).

But the recipes are and always have been either the brainchild of or super- vised by Susan Massaron, this time aided by Judy Doherty and Juan Gonzales. Susan spoils our taste buds while keeping us thin and healthy.

The published Pritikin research is completely the result of our fortuitous association with Dr. James Barnard. My father always said that if it weren't for Jim we would never have published results.

And thanks to all of my editors: Dr. Bill McCarthy, Maria McIntosh, R.D., Dr. Jay Kenney, and Jim Barnard. Thanks also to April Murphy, Denise Coso, Lorraine Tiffany-Malone, Rita Swafford, and my literary agent Angela Miller for believing in me.

Special thanks to my brother Ken, who lost 45 pounds on the concept, and who has been a true confidant and architect in the development of my father's vision.

And no acknowledgment would be accurate without mentioning Kevin Wiser, who constantly motivates me and keeps me honest. And of course my mother, Ilene, and my wife, Christine, for being my biggest fans.

Time-Life Books is a division of Time Life Inc.

TIME LIFE INC.
PRESIDENT and CEO   Jim Nelson

TIME-LIFE TRADE PUBLISHING
VICE PRESIDENT and PUBLISHER   Neil Levin
Senior Director of Acquisitions
and Editorial Resources   Jennifer Pearce
Director of New Product Development   Carolyn Clark
Director of Trade Sales   Dana Coleman
Director of Marketing   Inger Forland
Director of New Product Development   Teresa Graham
Director of Custom Publishing   John Lalor
Director of Special Markets   Robert Lombardi
Director of Design   Kate L. McConnell

THE PRITIKIN PRINCIPLE
Director of Creative Services   Laura McNeill
Editor for Special Markets   Anna Burgard
Technical Specialist   Monika Lynde
Production Manager   Vanessa Hunnibell
Quality Assurance   Jim King, Stacy L. Eddy
Design   Universal Communications

Pre-Press Services, Time-Life Imaging Center
Printed in the United States
10 9 8 7 6 5 4 3 2

TIME-LIFE is a trademark of Time Warner Inc., and affiliated
companies.

ISBN 0-7370-1616-7

CIP data available upon application:
Librarian, Time-Life Books
2000 Duke Street
Alexandria, VA 22314

Books produced by Time-Life Trade Publishing are available at a
special bulk discount for promotional and premium use. Custom
adaptations can also be created to meet your specific marketing goals.
Call 1-800-323-5255.

TABLE OF CONTENTS

INTRODUCTION

Get ready to change your ideas about weight loss. Those of you who
believe that weight loss has to include hunger—that you have to starve
yourself in order to lose a few pounds—are about to learn otherwise. Those
who believe that you have to eat a lot of high-protein foods, loaded with fat
and cholesterol, in order to lose weight are about to be disabused of such a
belief. Those who think that a whole array of low-fat foods—including
such stalwarts as popcorn and whole-grain breakfast cereals—are good for
weight loss are about to be disillusioned. And those who believe that the
most effective weight loss programs are highly restrictive and impossible to
sustain are about to be pleasantly surprised. As I say, many of your ideas
about losing weight are going to change.

That's not all that will change as you read this book. For those of you
who are familiar with the Pritikin Program, get ready to change your per-
ception of us, as well. The Calorie Density Solution presents a set of
principles that transcend many of our old, fundamental assumptions about
diet, weight, and health. In certain cases, it reaffirms some long-held
beliefs, but only after coming at them from an entirely new perspective. In
other cases, it alters them entirely.

As you know, the weight loss industry is many decades old, so it's a little hard to believe that something altogether new and illuminating was still
out there waiting to be discovered. But the truth is, there was. A set of
principles that transcended virtually all we know about weight loss was still
out there, buried in the bushes, so to speak. Upon reflection, it shouldn't
be too hard to believe that something entirely new and enlightening still

waited to be discovered. After all, weight loss programs have been failing since they were created. Something had to be wrong with them. Although you won't see me wasting a lot of time and energy describing what's wrong with other programs, you will understand why weight loss programs have failed after you understand the Calorie Density Solution. More important, you'll know how and why a weight loss program can work.

The Calorie Density Solution is the most precise and simple program available. Essentially, it identifies the relative concentration of calories in a particular food. As you will see, we have created a system in which all foods can be compared for their calorie concentration or density. By knowing which foods are a source of concentrated calories, versus those that are low in calorie density, you can choose foods that promote weight loss. As you will see in the pages that follow, certain foods are not only low in calorie concentration, but they also fill you up. These foods create satiety before you have eaten too many calories—a combination that's great for weight loss.

In an unexpected and ironic way, the calorie density principle underlies most effective weight loss programs, even when the proponents of those programs didn't realize they were utilizing the principles of calorie density. As they promoted their diets using some gimmick or new principle, many of these same programs relied on foods that were low in calorie concentration in order to promote weight loss. In effect, they employed the calorie density principles, albeit unwittingly and in a rudimentary and imprecise way.

Let me give you an example. Proponents of many high-protein diets today encourage you to eat foods rich in protein, fat, and cholesterol. At the same time, they restrict your carbohydrate consumption. They tell you not to eat brown rice, pasta, bread, bagels, dried cereals, and carrots. Not surprisingly, some people who religiously follow these programs find themselves losing weight, at least initially. Pretty soon, however, many people also discover that their health is deteriorating rapidly as a result of this rich diet. They also find themselves craving carbohydrate-rich foods. Eventually, those cravings become intolerable and cause a binge on bread, bagels, pastries, or some other carbohydrate-rich food. Shortly thereafter, the person discovers that he's off the diet and has regained all the weight that he initially lost. He's probably gained a few additional pounds, as well.

Yet, there was truth to what the high-protein proponents were saying. Unfortunately, that truth was buried in the midst of so much confusion and misinformation. In fact, certain carbohydrate foods *do* cause you to gain weight—not because *all* carbohydrates cause weight gain, but because some carbohydrate foods have been dried and processed and consequently have had their calories packed together, or concentrated. As you will see in the pages that follow, these foods have a very high calorie density and do cause weight gain. That is not the case, however, with many other carbohydrate-rich foods. Brown rice and carrots, for example, will help promote *weight loss*. In fact, they will fill your stomach on relatively few calories.

Up until now, identifying foods that cause weight loss or weight gain has been like firing an unguided missile. Sometimes, on rare occasions, it hits the target, but mostly it hits innocent bystanders, which is precisely why the vast majority of diets fail.

I apply this uncompromising truth even to our own program. For more than 20 years, we focused primarily on lowering fat and cholesterol in the diet, while increasing carbohydrates and other plant-based nutrients. Because we were so focused on these constituents, we overlooked foods that had their calories concentrated. Therefore, we encouraged people to eat whole-grain bread, for example, or whole-grain bagels—foods that promote weight gain. We even served popcorn—another source of concentrated calories—in the auditorium where we showed our movies at night. Why not? we said. They're low in fat and they have no cholesterol. Unfortunately, these foods had their calories concentrated. They were calorically dense.

To be fair, it was easy for us—and everyone else—to make this mistake. No one had recognized calorie density as yet. Well, actually one person did recognize it: my father, Nathan Pritikin. He wrote about it back in 1973 and again in his book, *The Pritikin Permanent Weight Loss Manual* (1981). He even used the term "calorie density" in that book. However, my father chose not to emphasize this aspect of the diet because, in those days, his primary concerns were fat and cholesterol—concerns that were appropriate even for weight loss.

When my father first began using his diet to treat disease, people were gaining weight because they ate too much fat, not because they ate carbohydrate-rich foods whose calories had been concentrated. In fact, there weren't that many concentrated carbohydrate foods available in those days. If you were going to avoid fat and eat carbohydrates back in the 1970s and early '80s, most of your foods would have to be unprocessed whole grains, vegetables, beans, and fruit—foods whose calories had not been concentrated. As you will see as you read this book, these foods have a very low-to-moderate calorie density. They promote weight loss.

A lot changed in the 1980s and '90s, however. Once food manufacturers realized that consumers wanted low-fat, low-cholesterol foods, they started producing myriad types of processed fare that, indeed, were low in fat and low in cholesterol. Unfortunately, these foods were also calorically dense because they had had their calories concentrated during processing.

People ate these foods in abundance, thinking they were good for their health and weight. As it turned out, a lot of people found weight loss impossible on diets rich in these foods, and many—perhaps most—even gained weight on such diets.

I am very happy to report that we have finally found a tool that can guide people to effective and efficient weight loss. By using the calorie density principle, you will be able to eat until you are full and still lose weight. On this program, I even encourage you to eat often—that is, three substantial meals, plus at least two snacks each day. Using the calorie density principle, you will discover that even as you fill your stomach, you will lose weight. This program is clear, simple, and easy to follow. This time, weight loss has been done right.

As with all our other books, this one is based on current medical science. Moreover, all the ideas outlined in this book have been tested at the Pritikin Longevity Center, in Santa Monica, California. We use our program to help people prevent and overcome heart disease, high blood pressure, adult-onset diabetes, obesity, and many other serious disorders.

More than 70,000 people have come to the Pritikin Longevity Centers in Santa Monica, Florida, and other locations, since they opened in 1976. The effectiveness of our program as a treatment for these and other illnesses is unparalleled and unmatched by any other publicly available health and weight loss program on the market today.

As you may know, the Pritikin Longevity Center at Santa Monica is not just health clinic, but a research center where scientists study the effects of diet and exercise on health. Scientists from the University of California at Los Angeles (UCLA) and other leading research centers have reported the effectiveness of our program in many of the world's leading medical journals.

Some of the findings reported by scientists who have examined the effects of our program on Pritikin participants include the following:

- The average drop in blood cholestrol levels among those studied was 23 percent.

- The majority of people studied who came to the Longevity Center suffering from acute chest pain left the center pain-free. Not only were they walking again, but many were now running.

- The vast majority of those studied—70 percent, to be exact—who came to our center with adult-onset diabetes and on oral medication left the center with normal blood sugar and off all medication. Forty percent who came taking insulin left insulin-free.

- Of those studied with high blood pressure and taking medication, 83 percent left our center with normal blood pressure and off all medication.

- Those with certain high risk factors for common cancers—breast, colon, and prostate—were able to cut those risk factors in half by the time they left the center.

- Those who were overweight lost weight, very often with dramatic results; yet, they never had to count calories or be hungry in order to lose weight.

Hundreds of people who suffered from obesity and who adopted the Pritikin Program have now achieved a healthy weight and have had no trouble maintaining it. Millions more have read our books and have had the same results as those demonstrated at the Longevity Center.

You do not have to come to the Pritikin Longevity Centers to experience these same benefits yourself. All that you need to achieve a healthy weight, prevent disease, and overcome many common disorders is provided in this book.

Among the beauties of the Pritikin Program's Calorie Density Solution is that it will promote weight loss, without hunger, while it helps to restore your health. In other words, this is a complete program. It is also very easy to maintain, which means it will help you sustain the good health and weight loss you achieve.

Moreover, you can follow this program and still travel, socialize, and enjoy a wide variety of common foods. Not only will I show you how to adhere to the program in virtually every situation, but I will also show you how you can eat foods that are richer in calorie density and still promote weight loss.

This program, unlike any other, provides maximum flexibility as you lose weight and regain your health. For that reason, as well as many others, this is the most effective weight loss program ever presented.

Robert Pritikin
Santa Monica, California
November 1999

1 | CALORIE DENSITY: THE KEY TO LONG-TERM WEIGHT LOSS AND GOOD HEALTH

The minute you pick up this book and start reading these words, you begin wrestling with a fundamental question, which is this: Can this program, or any other, succeed in helping me achieve good health and the weight I want?

Allow me to make your decision a little easier by establishing a set of criteria that can help you evaluate any diet and health program. If a program is to succeed at helping you restore your ideal weight, good health, and youthful appearance, it must:

- Offer a food plan that you can enjoy and maintain, with pleasure, for the rest of your life.

- Give you the freedom to eat until you are full and never limit your portions or be hungry in order to lose weight.

- Encourage you to eat frequently, including three meals a day and two or three snacks per day.

- Allow you to dine out in restaurants and travel throughout the world without having to go off the program.

- Promote your health, give you high energy, a more youthful appearance, prevent disease, and enhance your chances of living a long, active life.

- Efficiently and effectively promote weight loss; help you achieve a healthy weight; and keep any excess weight off without hunger.

Notice that I placed weight loss as the final standard by which a successful program must be measured. I did this for a very simple reason: All weight loss programs work—at least intially. The reason is simple: Causing initial loss of weight is the easy part. All you have to do is devise a program that causes you to eat fewer calories than you burn each day as energy. In fact, you could lose weight, at least temporarily, by following the all-celery diet. And no doubt when that book is written, there will be people who will come forward and tell you they lost 50 pounds on the all-celery program. But what happens to those people a few months or a year down the road? The vast majority of them regain all the weight they lost and then add on additional pounds. The real test for any diet-and-health program is not whether a regimen causes short-term weight loss, but whether it can be sustained and enjoyed, whether it can boost your health, restore your youthful appearance, and give you the freedoms I describe above.

The most common reasons for abandoning weight loss diets are: first, the diet is too restrictive; second, it's unpalatable; third, it harms the person's health, makes him or her feel terrible, and perhaps even leads to serious illness.

Once people realize that they cannot stay on a diet, they go back to their old ways of eating. Unfortunately, by the time that happens, they feel so deprived and hungry that they are possessed by intense cravings for the foods that they once enjoyed, especially foods rich in calories, such as processed foods and those rich in fat and sugar. Naturally, such rich foods cause people to gain back all the weight they lost while dieting and sometimes many additional pounds.

In the face of such failures, many people have simply given up dieting. They indulge in what is now being called the "pleasure revenge," meaning they allow themselves to gorge on fat, processed foods, and sugar, which just makes them fatter and sicker. In the end, the pleasure revenge backfires.

Other people try instead to improve their diets by limiting their fat intake while increasing their consumption of carbohydrate-rich foods. On the surface, this makes good sense, since a gram of fat contains 9 calories, while a gram of carbohydrate contains only 4 calories. By limiting fat, you should be able to limit the calories you take in. That should cause weight loss. Or so you would think.

But the more common experience among people who simply limit fat but eat more carbohydrate-rich foods is that they can't lose weight, or they gain additional pounds. Now that's frustrating!

You follow what seems like the best advice available and you still get fat! Which is why so many of us believe that it doesn't matter what we do; there's no way we're going to lose weight permanently. We might as well eat fat, sugar, and all the processed foods we want because, in the end, we're still going to be overweight and sick.

Somehow, by some triumph of the human spirit, millions of us remain optimistic and attempt one more diet and health program. Every year, about half the adults in America are on some kind of weight reduction plan. On any given day, about 40 percent of women and 20 percent of men say they are trying to lose weight. They carry on in the hope that they will lose weight and regain some of their youthful vitality and appearance. Most of these people are veterans of other diets and many are yo-yo dieters, meaning they are regularly on and off weight loss programs. Unfortunately, what they experience more than anything else is continual failure.

The program I describe in this book will help you experience the success you have been searching for. It's called the Pritikin Program, which now uses a very powerful new tool called the Calorie Density Solution. The Calorie Density Solution offers you a diet that is delicious and highly flexible; you will be able to eat as much as you want of this diet, as often as you desire, and still lose weight. You'll be able to eat in restaurants and travel. I will even show you how, within certain limits, you'll be able to cheat without gaining weight or becoming ill. This program, with all of these built-in freedoms, can help you achieve your healthy weight and experience better health. It can even be used to prevent or treat many serious diseases. In order to achieve these goals, you must fully understand and utilize a single principle that can guide you to your desired weight in virtually any situation you find yourself. As you will soon see, the calorie density principle is the single, most effective tool for weight loss ever discovered.

CALORIE DENSITY: THE STORY BEHIND WEIGHT

Allow me to begin my description of calorie density by relating a little allegory. Let's imagine that two little towns live side by side and each subsists on foods that are direct opposites from the other. One town lives on a type of food that is extremely dense; these foods contain an abundance of calories that are packed tightly together. Their diet is so dense with calories, in fact, that you might even call it calorie-lead. The other town lives on a very different type of food, one that is porous, light, and low in calories. There was no commerce between the two towns and neither one knew much about the other.

The people who ate the calorically dense diet loved their foods, but found that very early in life most became overweight. Eventually, they also became sick and impaired. Many died prematurely. One day, a smart salesperson came along and told the townspeople that in order to lose weight and be healthy again, they had to start eating less food. The people thought that he was probably right and started limiting the amount of food they ate. As a result, many lost weight, but most of them could not endure the hunger that resulted from eating less. They hated being hungry; they also hated having to discipline their natural instinct to eat. So even after they lost weight and felt better, their discipline snapped and eventually they went back to their old ways of eating. Pretty soon, they gained back all their lost weight and became heavier and sicker than they were before.

In the neighboring town, the people had developed a cuisine based on foods that were calorically light. They loved their food, too—in fact, they loved their food just as much as the people who ate the calorically dense food did. However, the people who ate the calorically light cuisine were naturally lean, healthy, and more energetic than their heavier neighbors. They never worried about eating too much. They didn't realize it, but these people were filling up their stomachs on very few calories. That allowed them to eat as much as they wanted, and as often as they wanted.

One day, a party of people from the town with the calorically light diet became curious and decided to do the unthinkable—they decided to visit the people of the neighboring town, whom they had never met before. When the two groups encountered each other, they marveled at how different each was from the other, especially in weight and appearance. Unfortunately, because neither side understood why they were so different, neither side could explain why one group of people was fat and sick and the other lean and healthy. In the end, each side decided that it must be their genes. We're just different, the two sides agreed. You lean and healthy people are lucky; we overweight and sick people are unlucky. That's the way it goes. No one realized that the major difference between the peoples was the caloric density of their respective diets.

CALORIE DENSITY: THE SECRET TO WEIGHT LOSS

Calorie density, as you no doubt have gathered, simply means the number of calories packed into a given weight of food. Certain foods have more calories packed into them—ounce for ounce or pound for pound—than others. That means that each food has its own calorie density. In order to compare the calorie density of different foods, we have to use the same weight when we compare them. We could use calories per ounce or calories per pound. It doesn't matter. Both would give the basis for a fair comparison. As you will see, we have chosen calories per pound.

The effect of a given food on your weight—whether it will likely increase your weight or decrease it—depends to a large extent on the number of calories packed into that food. The higher the caloric density, the more likely a food is to cause weight gain, while the lower a food's caloric density, the more likely it is to cause weight loss.

Weight loss is achieved by following a very simple axiom: eat fewer calories than you burn each day. A calorie is the unit of measure for energy. If you eat fewer calories than you burn as energy, your body will start drawing from your reserve calories, most of which are stored in the form of fat. This will cause you to lose weight. On the other hand, if you consume more calories than you burn, the extra calories will be stored in your body, primarily as fat.

Weight loss is accelerated as you increase activity, simply because you're burning more energy as you increase your activity levels. Exercise, therefore, tends to promote weight loss, unless, of course, you increase the number of calories you eat.

This is where calorie density comes in. In general, if you eat a diet that is calorically dense, or rich in calories, you're much more likely to gain weight, especially if you do not exercise. Moreover, if the foods in your diet are sufficiently dense with calories—caloric-lead, you might say—you're going to gain weight, no matter how much exercise you do.

People who eat a calorie-dense diet but want to lose weight will have to eat very small portions of food in order to keep their calories down. That means, of course, that they will be hungry most of the time, just like one set of townspeople in my example.

On the other hand, if you eat a diet that is calorically light, you will lose weight. In fact, if the foods you eat are sufficiently low in calorie density, you could eat all day long and still lose weight, especially if you also do some moderate amount of exercise, such as taking a daily walk.

As I said, food varies dramatically in calorie density. For example, most processed foods—especially those that have been dried—have a very high calorie density. The calories in these foods have been concentrated during drying and processing.

Foods that contain significant amounts of fat also have a higher than average calorie density. As you may know, many of the foods in your local supermarket have been dried and contain fat. The calories in these foods are highly concentrated, which means they are virtually guaranteed to cause weight gain in most people.

On the other hand, unprocessed whole grains, vegetables, beans, and fruit are low in calorie density. Many animal foods, such as fish and certain lean cuts of beef, are moderate in calorie density.

As you will see, there are also low-calorie dense processed foods that will contribute to weight loss. Oatmeal is a good example, providing only 280 calories per pound. Whole-wheat pasta is moderately low in calorie density, providing 560 calories per pound. It also contains fiber and is rich in nutrients. Fiber, as we will see, plays a significant role in filling you up and cutting down on the calories you consume. White pasta, on the other hand, is higher in calorie density than whole wheat, providing 630 calories per pound. Both forms of pasta can contribute to weight gain, though white pasta is far more likely to add on the pounds. (Later in the book, I will show you how you can lower the calorie density of both whole-wheat and white pasta to make the food far less likely to cause weight gain.)

Here's a chart to show the calorie densities of some foods.

CALORIE DENSITY

FOOD	CALORIES PER POUND
PLANT FOODS	
Lettuce	65
Broccoli	130
Strawberries	140
Apple	270
Oatmeal, plain	280
Potato, baked	490
Brown rice, boiled	500
Yam, baked	525
Whole-wheat pasta	560
Black beans, cooked	600
FISH, SEAFOOD, CHICKEN	
King crab	460
Orange roughy	400
Shrimp	630
Lobster	450
Cod	480
Halibut, poached	520
Chicken breast, no skin	750
Tuna, bluefin	830
Salmon, coho	810

CALORIE DENSITY *continued*

FOOD	CALORIES PER POUND

MEAT

Pork tenderloin	750
Top sirloin	870
Top round	950
Veal	980
Round, "prime"	975
Rib eye, "choice"	1,020

PROCESSED FOODS

Bread, white	1,210
Pretzels	1,770
Oreo cookies	2,200
Granola bar, hard	2,140
Pringles potato chips	2,550
Chocolate-chip cookies	2,140
Fats and oils	3,250 to
(e.g., butter, margarine, olive, corn, soybean margarine, lard)	4,100

As you can see, calorie density tends to be low among unprocessed plant foods. These foods derive their weight mostly from water, which of course contains no calories. In fact, foods that are proportionately rich in water—such as vegetables and fruit—or those that have been cooked in water—such as grains and beans—tend to be low to moderate in calorie density. Calorie density is also low to moderate among many animal foods, particularly those that are low in fat.

A water-rich diet, in fact, is common among Asian populations, such as the Japanese and Chinese, who eat diets proportionately rich in vegetables and cooked grains. This is one of the primary reasons why so many Asians are lean. Without explicitly stating it, Asian peoples are employing the calorie density principle.

In the West, more and more plant foods are creeping into the diet, but unfortunately most of these are processed and dried. Dried foods and processed foods that contain fat have much higher calorie densities. A comparison between the low and high ends of the spectrum demonstrates how extreme these differences can be. For example, one tablespoon of olive oil contains as many calories as a whole pound of cherry tomatoes, or steamed broccoli, or fresh strawberries.

As the allegory from page 3 explains—and the chart confirms—there really are two worlds of food, one that is high in calorie density and another that is low. In fact, there is a great divide among our foods today. On one hand, we have the high-calorie dense foods that most Americans now eat, including the high-fat fast foods that are so common today. On the other hand, we have whole, unprocessed plant foods, as well as low-fat animal foods.

The problem is that, like the people in the two towns I described, most of us simply don't realize this fact. Consequently, we make the mistake of consuming diets that are made up largely of high-calorie dense foods. Naturally, such a diet causes weight gain and illness. As a general rule, the closer a given food is to its natural state, the more likely its calorie density will be low.

WHY CALORIES PER POUND

Before I go any further, allow me to say why I choose to use "calories per pound" as a standard measure. First, calories per pound levels the playing field among all foods. I realize that you are not going to eat a pound of most foods at a single meal. However, calories per pound allows you to compare all foods for their calorie content, or density, using the same measuring stick. It's easier to picture a pound of food, as opposed to, say, an ounce or a gram. We could just as easily have said calories per ounce, or calories per gram, and used that to compare the varying calorie densities of foods. The only problem with calories per ounce, or calories per gram, is that very few people—myself included—know what an ounce feels like, or even more difficult, a gram. As I tell people in my classes, I always put on extra postage stamps, because I'm really not sure what an ounce feels like.

A pound, on the other hand, is familiar. A big bag of chips is a pound of food. Most of the items we buy in bulk, such as brown rice, beans, vegetables, and fruit, are priced and purchased by the pound. The hardcover edition of this book weighs about a pound. By knowing the calories per pound, we can compare very different kinds of foods—broccoli, potatoes, flounder, and hamburger meat, for example—for their potential effects on your weight.

Calories per pound gives us a "real-world" way of comparing the relative calorie contents of very different foods. It's as simple as that.

However, once you understand the calories-per-pound concept, you can then compare the calorie densities of whole meals. That's what is really important because it's the average calorie density of your overall diet that best predicts whether your diet will cause weight loss or weight gain. In most cases, you're not eating just one food when you sit down to a meal. You're eating several foods and all of them may have very different calorie densities. Therefore, you want to know the average calorie density of your entire meal in order to know how that meal will affect your weight. I show you how to do that in the next chapter.

In Chapter 6, I list the calorie density of virtually every common food. You can use these figures to understand the relative calorie densities—and the effects of each food—on your weight. It's important for you to have a good idea of the relative calorie densities of various foods, especially when you are learning the system, but as I will show you in Chapters 2 and 3, you don't have to know the exact calorie densities in order to make this system work for you.

MAKE YOUR STOMACH HAPPY, AS YOU LOSE WEIGHT

Hunger is a natural and essential part of our instinct to survive. Whenever you consciously restrict your food intake, your hunger drive triggers a very ancient and primitive survival mechanism that demands that you fill up on as many calories as you can in order to go on living. This instinct arose out of our ancestors' repeated experience with food shortages and famines. Nature programmed us genetically to eat as much as possible whenever we experience real hunger. This response to hunger, in fact, is one of the reasons humans survived these past two million years. We were never designed to attempt to defeat our hunger drive. Yet, a great many weight loss programs ask us to do just that. It is a self-defeating act that, as most of us have experienced, eventually fails.

Instead of fighting our hunger and trying to repress it, we should embrace it. If we accept that we are designed to satisfy our hunger, we'll have to ask ourselves an important question: How can I fill up my stomach, satisfy my hunger, and still lose weight? In fact, that question leads directly to the solution for weight loss and good health.

Your stomach holds between two and three pounds of food. The feeling of fullness is created largely by the volume of your food. Volume has little to do with the number of calories in your food. There's no little accountant down there making sure you get a certain number of calories before you feel full. On the contrary, your stomach doesn't care if you've got 500 calories in the food you eat, or a thousand. What matters is that it feels full or sated.

WATER AND FIBER: FILLING THE
STOMACH WITHOUT CAUSING WEIGHT GAIN

A meal can have a large volume but low calorie density. Indeed, this is exactly the case with vegetables, fruit, beans, and natural, unprocessed grains. These foods are low to moderate in calorie density. Yet, they create tremendous feelings of fullness, or satiety, in your stomach.

The factors that create volume, or bulk, and thus create feelings of fullness, are water and fiber, neither of which have any calories. Foods that contain a lot of water and/or fiber, therefore, tend to be lower in calorie density. Yet, they have a high satiety value. In other words, they have a great capacity to create feelings of fullness and satisfaction, while providing relatively few calories.

Take broccoli or potatoes, for example, both of which have too much volume, or bulk—thanks to their water and fiber content—for us to be able to eat a full pound of them. But even if you did eat a pound of broccoli, you'd only be getting 130 calories. If you ate a pound of baked potatoes, you'd only be consuming 490 calories.

In fact, a potato has about the same number of calories as a slice of bread, believe it or not. Yet, they create very different feelings of fullness. Eat a potato and you're going to feel full, or close to it, but eat a single slice of bread and you'll be looking for more food—and more calories. The same is true for fresh fruit versus dried fruit. Fresh apples have a calorie density of 270 calories per pound, while dried apples have a calorie density of 1,100 calories per pound. A single apple is usually satisfying, but many people can finish off a bag of dried fruit—and still not feel full or satisfied. Foods that contain water and fiber are far more filling than those that are dried or processed.

You very likely experience this same phenomenon whenever you eat at a Chinese restaurant. You eat a big Chinese meal, with lots of vegetables and steamed rice and feel stuffed to the top of your neck. Because the meal you just ate was high in water and fiber, it was still low in calories. This is why you may have felt hungry two hours after you finished the meal. Your body needs energy so it signals you to eat. If you then eat another meal that contains plenty of water and fiber and is low in calorie density, you will be full again for two or three hours. You will also be hungry again a few hours later. Because you know how to select foods for their calorie density, you could eat another meal that fills you up but is low in calorie density. You'd be full again, but guess what: You'd very likely be losing weight.

Now I know what you're thinking, especially those of you who have been calorie counters. What's the difference, you may be wondering, if you eat a big meal that's loaded with calories but the meal fills you up for, say, four hours? Wouldn't two calorically dense meals per day provide you with the same number of calories as three or four calorically light meals over those same 12 hours? The answer is no. Research has shown that at the end of the day, two or three calorically dense meals provide more calories overall than, say, three calorically light meals and two calorically light snacks. If you follow the Pritikin Program, you will be eating four or five times a day and still losing weight.

One of the reasons for this phenomenon is that meals composed of low-calorie dense foods fill your stomach on significantly fewer calories than meals composed of high-calorie dense foods. That means that, overall, your total calorie food intake will be lower on the three calorically light meals and two snacks than it would on the two calorically heavy meals. A day's worth of low-calorie dense foods will cause you to feel full and satisfied, while they promote weight loss and improved health.

Interestingly, high-calorie dense foods—those that have little moisture, are rich in fat, or both—tend to have low satiety value, meaning it takes a lot of these foods to create a feeling of fullness. Potato chips are a good example. It's not unheard of for people to eat half of a one-pound bag of potato chips, which amounts to 1,200 calories. Add some type of onion dip and a couple of beers and you've consumed enough calories at one sitting for a whole day. And we haven't even counted the rest of your day's meals yet.

Obviously, it takes a lot more calories from calorically dense foods to satisfy your appetite and that's the problem. Many overweight people will tell you how little they eat but the truth is that they eat small amounts of foods with very high calorie densities. They don't have to eat a lot of those foods in order to consume a lot of calories and promote weight gain.

Ideally, you want to eat a diet that is composed mostly of low-calorie dense foods, which will allow you to fill up on the fewest calories possible. Not only will this cause weight loss, but it will also give you maximum freedom to enjoy a wider and more varied diet. If the vast majority of your foods are exceedingly low in calorie density, you will have the freedom to occasionally enjoy a high-calorie dense food—without having to worry about weight gain.

That, in essence, is the Pritikin Program's Calorie Density Solution.

PROCESSING AND FAT: WHERE THE CALORIES ARE CONCENTRATED

The epidemic spread of overweight and obesity is essentially a modern phenomenon. Half the adult U.S. population is now overweight or obese and the number of people falling into these categories is increasing each year. The percentage of the world's population that is overweight today is greater than at any other time in human history. The question is, Why? The short answer is that we are consuming more calorie dense foods than ever before. Meanwhile, we are increasingly sedentary. The overabundance of calories is coming primarily from two places: fat and foods that have had their calories concentrated during processing.

Throughout the 1970s and '80s, the primary health concern in the American diet was fat, and with good reason, since it was linked with high rates of heart disease, cancer, adult-onset diabetes, and obesity. In fact, the relative amount of fat in the average American diet has fallen somewhat during the past two decades. Fat is still a major health concern, but an insidious and pervasive trend occurred in the 1990s that gave fat an accomplice as a threat to health and ideal weight. That trend was massive food processing.

When a food is processed, its calories have been concentrated because the water has been removed along with some or all of the fiber. The calories in the food are packed together into a smaller weight and volume.

For example, in its unprocessed state, corn contains about 490 calories per pound. Though many people don't realize it, corn kernels still contain water. They also have fiber. Water provides no calories. Soluble fiber provides minute amounts and insoluble fiber none at all. Yet, both water and fiber do provide bulk, which fills your stomach. This is why I say that unprocessed foods are low in calorie density, but high in satiety value. They fill you up on relatively low amounts of calories.

When corn kernels are dried and ground up to make tortillas, the calories in the corn have been concentrated, or bunched tightly together. It takes many more corn particles to occupy the same volume that the actual corn kernels filled before. Consequently, those corn tortillas now contain 1,000 calories per pound. Dry and grind that corn meal even finer so that even more calories can be packed together and you've got corn flakes, with 1,770 calories per pound. The processed tortillas and corn flakes are now packed with calories; they are much more calorically dense than the original corn.

Many processed foods also contain added fat, the most calorically dense substance in the food supply. As I said earlier, fat contains 9 calories per gram, carbohydrates and protein, only 4 calories per gram. When you add fat to corn flour and fry it to make corn chips, you've now got a food that contains 2,450 calories per pound.

But even dried food with no added fat can be extremely high in caloric density. Pretzels, regarded by many people as a healthy snack because they are largely fat-free, provide 1,770 calories per pound. Air-popped popcorn is also low in fat and considered by many to be good for weight loss, but it provides 1,730 calories per pound. That's the same as a pound of white sugar. "How can that be?" one participant at the Pritikin Longevity Center asked me. Popcorn has fiber and bulk. It should fill up your stomach on relatively few calories. The trouble with popcorn is that we chew it and, in the process, compress the fibrous puffs into tiny bits of food, which in turn allows a lot of popcorn—and a lot of calories—to enter your stomach before you are full. Popcorn, it turns out, contains more calories per pound than cheesecake, which provides 1,440 calories per pound! The cheesecake has no fiber, but it does contain water, which the popcorn and pretzels do not.

Today, supermarkets are flooded with foods that are low in fat, high in carbohydrates, and extremely high in calories. These include many obvious foods, such as "fat-free" cookies, cakes, chips, muffins, as well as many not-so-obvious weight-boosters, such as dried cereals, bread, granola bars, trail mix, and crackers. Many people eat dried cereal as a snack every night, thinking that because these foods are considered "whole grains" and are low in fat, they are good for weight loss. On the contrary, most dried cereals provide between 1,130 and 2,210 calories per pound. Like the proverbial wolves in sheep's clothing, a lot of these foods look absolutely innocuous. Snackwell Cookie Cakes, for example, contain 0 percent fat. Unfortunately, they also provide 1,420 calories per pound. Likewise, Wow Potato Chips contain no fat, but still have 1,220 calories per pound.

As I said, not all processed foods are bad for weight loss, however. Those that are moist or have been cooked in water and contain fiber tend to be low in calorie density. Two excellent examples are whole-wheat pasta, which contains only 560 calories per pound—still a relatively low-calorie dense food—and cooked oatmeal, which contains 280 calories per pound.

It's important to keep in mind, therefore, that there are good processed foods and bad, some that will promote weight loss, and others that will cause weight gain. If we are to be successful at achieving a healthy weight and good health, we must know the difference.

WHY EVEN THE WELL-INTENTIONED ARE GAINING WEIGHT

The consequence of the increased reliance upon processed foods, coupled with our concerns over fat, has given rise to widespread confusion about the effects of food on weight and health, even among people who are concerned and try to be well informed. People have been trying to reduce their fat intake in order to lose weight and promote their health. Instead of eating high-fat foods, they have switched to high-carbohydrate foods. Unfortunately, all too often those high-carbohydrate foods have a calorie density that is as high, or nearly as high, as the high-fat foods that people are now trying to avoid. Therefore, they are gaining weight.

Foods low in fat no longer can be considered automatically good for weight loss. In fact, some are worse than those rich in fat. This is one of the primary reasons why Americans are still gaining weight, even as they attempt to avoid fatty foods. They fail to realize that foods low in fat and cholesterol may also be high in calories.

There is a solution and it's easier than you might think.

LOW CALORIE DENSITY DIET — MADE EVEN LOWER

The first step to losing weight without ever being hungry is to eat a diet that is low in calorie density. But you can lower the calorie density of your meals simply by *adding* certain low-calorie dense foods.

As I will show in greater detail in Chapter 3, the calorie density of a meal—even a meal with some dried or processed foods—can be lowered when it is combined with foods that have a low calorie density. If you add strawberries to oatmeal, for example, you will bring down its already-low calorie density. If you add vegetables to pasta—as in the case of pasta primavera—you will lower its calorie density, as well. A large salad with a low-calorie dense dressing can reduce the calorie density of a restaurant meal, as can a dessert with fresh berries and sherbet.

Such additions reduce a meal's calorie density because they add bulk to your meal, which means that you feel full before you consume too many calories. Overall, you will eat less pasta if your linguine contains, say, asparagus, broccoli, carrots, kale, or collard greens. The fiber and water in these vegetables add bulk to the food and thus fill your stomach at a point when the actual calorie count will not be enough to maintain your current weight. You'll be full, but losing weight.

Adding salsa to bean dip is another example of lowering a food's calorie density by adding more food. The salsa has a very low calorie density. While it enhances the flavor of the bean dip, it also lowers the dip's calorie density significantly. Adding a salad and a vegetable to a meal brings down the meal's overall calorie density, as well, because these low-calorie dense meals fill you up before you've consumed a lot of calories.

This is to say nothing, of course, of the health benefits of such vegetables. Adding vegetables is, in fact, adding vitamins, minerals, phytochemicals, and fiber. They make you healthier as they promote weight loss.

What matters at the end of the day is whether the overall calorie density of your diet is low and rich in nutrients, or what I refer to as having "high nutrient density." We want the calorie density to be so low, in fact, that you consume fewer calories than you burn. As you progress through this book, you will see that this is not that difficult to achieve. In fact, lowering your calorie density very often means adding foods to your diet, rather than cutting them out. The trick, as I will explain shortly, is to fill your stomach and satisfy your tastebuds on as few calories as possible. That is the secret to weight loss without hunger.

In general, this can be accomplished on a diet that is based primarily on plant foods, with smaller amounts of fish, lean cuts of meat, and non-fat dairy products. As you will see, such a diet can ensure weight loss, especially if you take a walk each day.

On the other hand, let's say that you ate a diet that was rich in fatty meats, bread, and other processed foods. You would have a diet that was high in caloric density, which would mean that you would very likely be gaining weight, especially if you did not do much exercise.

ACHIEVING TWO OF YOUR MOST CHERISHED GOALS

The Pritikin Program is designed to help you achieve both a healthy weight and good health. We want you to look good and feel great. We believe that any program that does not improve your health as it lowers your weight is doomed to fail. Therefore, we are going to teach you how to use the calorie density tool to achieve both these fundamental goals.

This program is especially effective for people suffering from overweight, obesity, and other degenerative diseases, such as adult-onset diabetes and coronary heart disease. As I will describe in great detail in Chapter 9 of this book, adult-onset diabetes arises from over-consumption of calories and lack of exercise. The condition, also referred to as metabolic overload, can be effectively controlled, and in many cases reversed, with a diet that is low in calorie density and high in nutrient density, along with daily exercise. The exercise program I recommend mostly involves taking a daily walk. Strenuous, heart-pounding exercise is not necessary for weight loss.

THE PRITIKIN PROGRAM: LOW CALORIE DENSITY, HIGH NUTRIENT DENSITY

The majority of foods on the Pritikin Program are low in calorie density and rich in nutrients. While plant foods make up the largest portion of foods, the program does allow up to three and a half ounces of animal protein—a serving size about the size of a deck of cards—and two servings of nonfat milk products per day. The total daily allotment of, say, fish, chicken, or red meat can be eaten at a single meal, or in smaller portions in two or three meals. This is how traditional people throughout the world still eat animal foods—as small pieces of fish, chicken, or meat, mixed in with lots of vegetables. Animal foods are limited because they contain saturated fat and cholesterol which, when eaten in excess, are harmful to your health.

The Pritikin Program is not a singular set of rules, however, but a set of guidelines to help you choose foods that have a low calorie density and a high nutrient content. The program is a strategy to help you increase the percentage of fresh vegetables, whole grains, beans, low-fat animal foods, and fruit in your diet. Once you have the guidelines clearly established in your mind, you will be able to choose the foods that have a low calorie density and a high nutrient content in any situation. You will also know how to lower a meal's calorie density, and thus reduce its tendency to promote weight gain. Finally, you will discover how you can cheat on the program by including certain high-calorie dense foods—such as olive oil and avocados—and still lose weight.

If I were to state the Program's most essential parts, I would say that it consists of the following five recommendations:

1. Eat Whole, Unprocessed, and Natural Carbohydrate-Rich Foods. In general, this simply means eating whole, unprocessed grains, vegetables, and fruits. These "preferred carbohydrate-rich foods" include brown rice, millet, barley, and oats; a wide assortment of dark green lettuce, onions, potatoes, and squash; beans, including black turtle beans, chickpeas, lentils, lima beans, and pinto beans; and fruit, such as apples, pears, strawberries, and bananas. Some processed whole-grain foods, such as oatmeal, are also acceptable, because they are cooked in water, have low calorie density, and are highly nutritious. Foods with moderate calorie densities, such as whole-wheat and white pasta, can be added to your diet, as long as you combine them with vegetables, as pasta primavera, for example, which lower their calorie density.

   For the most efficient and maximum weight loss, you should avoid bread, rolls, bagels, and other flour products. When made from whole grains, they are highly nutritious and generally good for health. But because they have been dried and their calories concentrated, they can cause weight gain.

2. Eat Foods Low in Fat. The Pritikin Eating Plan includes smaller portions of beef, chicken, fish, and low-fat dairy products. We recommend that you eat no more than three and a half ounces of fish, poultry, or meat per day. In addition, we urge you to avoid fried foods, dressings with fat, and other sources of fat in your diet.

3. Eat Frequently. We encourage you to eat three full meals per day, along with two or three recommended snacks between meals. Hunger is the primary reason most diets fail. On the Pritikin Program, you are encouraged to eat whenever you are hungry.

4. Be Active. A sedentary lifestyle is linked to a wide array of disorders, including cardiovascular disease and some forms of cancer. In order to prevent illness and improve health, we recommend at least one 30-minute walk per day. If your current health and fitness allow, your walk should be at least two to three miles longer.

5. Avoid Salty Foods and Limit Salt Intake. High salt intake is associated with high blood pressure, the leading cardiovascular disease among Americans today.

As you will see in Chapter 5, these guidelines are coupled with three clearly articulated dietary plans, each one successively lower in calorie density and thus better at promoting weight loss and improving health. The three programs—labeled "Better," "Better Still," and "Best"—offer menus for seven days' worth of breakfasts, lunches, and dinners.

That, in summary, is the Pritikin approach. The Pritikin Program is the most effective diet-and-exercise approach ever created for overcoming heart disease, high blood pressure, adult-onset diabetes, overweight, and many other degenerative illnesses. If you follow the recommendations outlined in this book, you can regain your healthy weight, experience abundant energy, and, in many cases, restore normal function to vital organs. Many people with serious degenerative illnesses, such as heart disease, adult-onset diabetes, and high blood pressure, will find the symptoms of these illnesses disappearing. Those with circulatory disorders and joint pain will very likely experience a reduction or elimination of that pain. You'll likely sleep deeper and wake up more refreshed. By following this program, you may well slow the aging process. A growing body of evidence suggests that a healthy lifestyle will slow the decline of mental function and may even help prevent Alzheimer's disease. In short, this program can transform every aspect of your life.

The program can accomplish these goals without causing feelings of deprivation or hunger. Once you become accustomed to the Pritikin foods and start to experience their effects on your health, the quality of your life will improve dramatically.

MORE THAN WEIGHT LOSS

In 1994, Carol Ward's husband looked at her carefully one day and insisted that she get a medical checkup. Recently retired as a legal assistant, Carol just didn't look well. She weighed 185 pounds, was constantly fighting bouts of fatigue, and seemed to be aging far more rapidly than was normal, her husband told her. Reluctantly, Carol acquiesced to her husband's request. She had a full physical and blood analysis done by her physician. A week later, a nurse called to inform her that her blood cholesterol level was 260 milligrams per deciliter of blood (mg/dl)—dangerously high and at serious risk of causing a heart attack—and that her blood sugar was 147. "You know you're diabetic, don't you," the nurse told her. "Your blood sugar is very, very high." She was also more than 50 pounds overweight.

"I dropped the phone," Carol recalls.

Two months later, at her sister's insistence, she was enrolled in the Pritikin Longevity Center.

Carol was used to eating a rich diet whose flavors were based in fat and processed foods. By comparison, the Pritikin Eating Plan seemed bland—at least initially. "I didn't think I could do it," Carol recalled later. "But then one of the chefs sat down with me and whispered, 'You know, your taste buds change.' By the following week, everything started to taste better."

At the Longevity Center, Carol learned an endless number of ways to spice up her cooking and enhance the food's flavors. She also learned how to use health-promoting foods to change every aspect of her health—from her cholesterol and blood sugar levels to her weight.

Today, Carol is no longer considered diabetic. Her blood sugar levels are normal and she controls the disorder exclusively with her diet and daily exercise of walking and gardening. Her cholesterol level is 170 mg/dl, and she weighs 127 pounds.

Her weight fell far more rapidly and far easier than she ever believed it would. In fact, she initially had trouble keeping her weight at a level she was comfortable with. "My weight fell to 120 pounds and I started looking a little peaked so I stuffed myself for a while to get back to 127."

Stuffing herself as she loses weight is her normal behavior, Carol said. "My friends are surprised, even a little embarrassed, at the quantities of food I put away. Yet, as long as I'm eating the right things and exercising every day, I just don't gain weight."

2 | USING THE CALORIE DENSITY SOLUTION

When you first committed to losing weight, you probably thought that you had to keep your calorie intake below a certain number—say, 1,200 to 1,400 calories a day. There are a few ways of doing that. One of the most popular ways is simply to count and limit the number of calories you consume. In order to do that, you must know how many calories are in each food you eat. You also have to know how many calories are in a specific serving size of each food. That gets complicated, as you know, because portion sizes vary and it's difficult, if not impossible, to weigh each food you eat, especially if you're eating in restaurants a lot. Okay, you'll guess at the weight of each food. Still, at the end of every day, you'll have to add up the calories you've consumed to know if you're below that 1,200 or 1,400 figure. In order to reduce your calorie intake you'll have to limit the amount of food you eat, which means you're going to be hungry a lot of the time. Other symptoms arise: you're cold, irritable, and fatigued. So be it, you may have said to yourself. You're committed to losing weight. You'll just have to deal with the discomforts until the weight is off.

Unfortunately, there's more bad news. As you restrict calories, your biological survival mechanisms kick in, which automatically slow down your metabolic rate in order to conserve energy. Once that happens, you start burning calories at a slower rate than you were before you started dieting, which means it's far more difficult now to lose weight. Your body does this because it thinks it's being starved. As a way of preserving your life, it's holding on to every calorie it can.

At the same time, your hunger increases. Your body is demanding that you eat.

As if that were not bad enough, it turns out that your metabolic rate will remain at this slower rate until all the weight you previously had is regained. That means that you'll continue to suffer all the hunger pangs until you've regained your weight. Obviously, this is not the best approach to weight loss.

Another way of keeping your calorie intake down is to go on a high-protein diet, which requires you to eat primarily animal foods. The overabundance of high protein foods, in combination with very little carbohydrate, throws your body into an abnormal metabolic state called *ketosis* in which your appetite is suppressed. That, in turn, makes it easier for you to eat fewer calories.

You may have thought twice about adopting a high-protein diet because such programs are rich in fat and cholesterol and low in essential vitamins, minerals, antioxidants, and phytochemicals. So be it, you may have said. You were committed to losing weight. You would do whatever it takes.

So began the arduous journey to a lower weight. Did you succeed at your goal of achieving long-term weight loss? Probably not. Most people don't. It doesn't matter whether you choose the first system I described, typically referred to as calorie counting or portion control, or the second, the high-protein regimen. The vast majority of people fail on both systems. They are way too cumbersome, limiting, and unhealthy. Calorie counting requires you to defeat one of your most basic biological drives, hunger. That's impossible for the vast majority of people. High-protein programs require you to avoid your body's primary source of fuel, carbohydrates, as well as all those immune-boosting and cancer-fighting nutrients in plant foods. Many people feel terrible on such programs and their health suffers significantly in myriad ways.

Fortunately, neither system is necessary. You don't have to count up a day's worth of calories, nor must you be hungry all the time. Neither do you have to avoid the foods that are most beneficial to your energy levels and health. There's a better way to lose weight and improve your health. All you have to do is know the calorie density of the foods you eat and keep your average calorie density of each meal below a certain number. As long as you keep your average calorie density low, you can eat as much as you want and you'll still lose plenty of body fat and improve your health.

In this chapter, I'm going to show you how easy it is to do that.

CALORIE DENSITY PRINCIPLE: EFFECTIVE WEIGHT LOSS WITHOUT HUNGER

The first thing I want you to know is that the calorie density principle has already been proven scientifically to be highly effective at reducing calorie intake and promoting weight loss. I am going to show you how to use the calorie density principle to fill your stomach, while providing your body with insufficient calories to sustain your weight. Not only will this cause you to lose weight, but you can do it on a diet that you enjoy eating for its taste and variety.

In 1998, Scottish researcher R. J. Stubbs and his colleagues placed healthy young men on three different diets—one composed of foods with a low calorie density; a second composed of foods of medium calorie density; and a third composed of high-calorie dense foods. The men were followed for 16 days, during which time the scientists monitored their weight. None of the men knew which of the diets they were on, and all were allowed to eat as much as they wanted of each diet. There was no need to be hungry or to be disciplined.

Not surprisingly, only the men on the low-calorie dense diet lost weight. Those on the diet of medium caloric density saw no change in weight. The men on the diet of high caloric density gained weight. Stubbs found that calorie density alone was the single most important factor that determined calorie intake, weight loss, or weight gain.

Stubbs also found that a diet composed of processed carbohydrates, whose calories have been concentrated, is enough by itself to drive up caloric density and cause weight gain—even when such a diet is low in fat. His subjects didn't need to eat fat to gain weight; they could do it on dried and processed carbs. People who look at a food's percentage of fat are often missing the real source of weight gain: the concentrated calories found in processed foods. They fail to realize that calorie density is far more important than the percentage of fat alone in predicting weight gain—or weight loss.

It's true that fat content is still important from a health standpoint, especially since fat promotes heart disease, cancer, adult-onset diabetes, and other degenerative diseases. Moreover, fat drives up a food's calorie density and makes it more likely to increase your weight. But Stubbs showed that fat alone can no longer be considered the primary cause of overweight. Many processed and concentrated carbohydrates can be just as bad.

Stubbs wasn't finished. He then turned his attention to the common practice of counting calories.

DON'T COUNT CALORIES: JUST KNOW THE AVERAGE CALORIE DENSITY OF EACH MEAL

Stubbs and his co-workers found that it's not necessary to count calories at all. Instead, know the average calorie density of your meal—something I will show you how to do momentarily—and then keep that average below a certain number. That alone will ensure that you are losing weight.

If you know the calorie density of each food you eat in a meal, and then get the average calorie density for your entire meal, you can determine if that meal is going to promote weight gain or weight loss. You don't have to add up a day's worth of calories. On the contrary, you can know the effects of a meal on your weight even before you lift a fork to your mouth.

A SUDDEN INSPIRATION

For those of us at the Pritikin Longevity Center, this and other research triggered a series of revelations, among which were the following:

1. We realized that we could create an easy-to-use system that allows you to know the average calorie density of your meals. We also realized that we could design each meal to cause weight loss, without requiring you to be hungry.

2. Once we knew that, we realized that we could lower the calorie density of each meal—and thereby make it more likely to cause weight loss—by adding foods to each meal. That's right: adding them. People automatically think that weight loss programs work by eliminating foods and cutting back on the portions they eat. But we were able to create a set of techniques to bring down the average calorie density of meals—and thus cause you to lose weight—by adding foods to those meals. You could call this subtraction through addition.

3. After we started working with our program, we developed a short-cut method of making sure that your average calorie density is low, without having to know the average calorie density of your meals. In other words, we knew we could teach people how to recognize calorie density, without having to memorize any numbers, and keep them on a low-calorie dense diet that promotes weight loss. This system would work for people who want to lose weight as rapidly as possible and are willing to adhere strictly to the program.

4. Finally, we were also able to create a system with maximum flexibility that allowed people to cheat from time to time and still lose weight. In order to enjoy that flexibility, you have to understand how to use the calorie density principle to its fullest potential. Actually, the system is so easy that anyone can grasp it and use it in any situation—whether they are eating at home, in a restaurant, or at a party where there are lots of tempting high-calorie dense foods to be found. Even in the midst of the most decadent buffets, you can still lower the calorie density of your meals and maintain or lower your weight.

YOU'RE ONLY SATISFIED IF YOU'VE EATEN UNTIL YOU'RE FULL

A fundamental principle of the calorie density approach is that the only way you can lose weight and keep that weight off is if you are able to eat until you are full and satisfied. If you can't do that, then you're not going to experience long-term weight loss.

Whether you lose weight or gain it depends on what you fill your stomach with. There are lots of ways you can fill your stomach—you can do it by loading it with greasy cheeseburgers, French fries, and jelly beans, or you can fill it with salads, pasta, vegetables, fish, and low-calorie dense desserts. Both sets of foods are capable of filling you to satiety, but their respective effects on your weight will be very different, because they have very different calorie densities.

The calorie density principle shows you how to fill your stomach and yet provide your body with fewer calories than you burn. This causes weight loss.

YOUR STOMACH, THE FISH BOWL

We accomplish this by keeping the calorie density of your diet low, but also by teaching you how to combine foods to lower your meal's average calorie density. As Stubbs showed, you don't have to count calories in order to lose weight. All you have to do is to fill your stomach while keeping the average calorie density of each meal below a certain threshold number. You can keep the average calorie density of your meals low by adding low-calorie dense foods and by restricting high-calorie dense foods.

Perhaps the best way I can illustrate this is to ask you to imagine that your stomach is a small fish bowl. Let's say that you decided to fill your fish bowl with peanuts, a food with a very high calorie density (2,640 calories per pound). Obviously, by the time you fill up the fish bowl with all those peanuts, it's going to contain a lot of calories. You could also fill your fish bowl with bananas, which have a moderate calorie density (about 420 calories per pound).

But here's an interesting idea: What if you filled the same fish bowl only half-way with the peanuts and filled the other half with bananas, a food with a moderate calorie density. Now you've cut the calories from the peanuts in half by adding the bananas, a food with a calorie density that is much lower than the peanuts. The fish bowl is just as full, but the average calorie density when the two foods are combined is considerably less than when the peanuts alone filled the bowl. By filling the bowl with a food that has a lower calorie density—i. e., the bananas—you have reduced the

23

amount of room in your stomach for the peanuts. In effect, you've crowded out the food with the higher calorie density.

We use the calorie density principle to do the same thing with your stomach. We add foods that will fill up your stomach, but at the same time bring down a meal's average calorie density. If you know the calorie densities of the foods you eat, you can combine them so that higher calorie dense foods are compensated for by lower calorie dense foods, thus bringing down the average calorie density of the entire meal dramatically. By adding a salad and a vegetable to a meal that includes, say, a piece of fish, the meal's average calorie density will be brought down significantly, assuming, of course, that the salad and vegetable are not covered with fat. Add a piece of fruit and it will bring it down even further.

Of course, you should stop eating when you are full. Also, keep in mind that we encourage you to eat one of our recommended snacks between meals, which are also low in calorie density.

The trick is to combine foods to make each meal's average calorie density so low that it cannot support your current weight. In the process, you will lose weight, as you fill up your stomach throughout the day.

AVERAGE CALORIE DENSITY: HOW TO AVOID COUNTING CALORIES

In order to understand average calorie density a little better, allow me to use a couple of common foods that, when combined, actually bring down the calorie density of the overall meal. Let's say you want to eat a bowl of white pasta, which has a moderately high calorie density of 630 calories per pound. You like white pasta, you want to eat it, but you also want to lose weight. How can you have your pasta and eat it, too? That's where the Calorie Density Solution comes in. Add equal portions of pasta with a vegetable that has a low calorie density, such as Chinese cabbage, with a calorie density of 65 calories per pound; or broccoli with 130; or kale, which also has a calorie density of 130 calories per pound. Let's say you use Chinese cabbage. When you add the calorie densities of the pasta and the cabbage together and then divide by two, you get an average calorie density of below 350 calories per pound (347½ to be exact)—that is, as long as you combine equal portions of pasta and vegetables.

We have found that for people who exercise, a meal with an overall calorie density below 400 calories per pound will cause weight loss. Allow me to be more specific.

AVERAGE CALORIE DENSITY OF 400 PER MEAL OR LOWER WILL CAUSE WEIGHT LOSS

We have found that if you are exercising daily—which, as I have said, means that you are walking every day—and the average calorie density of your meals is 400 calories per pound, or less, you're likely to lose weight, no matter what your present weight may be.

Meals that provide an average calorie density of 400 calories per pound will fill up your stomach, but provide fewer calories than your body needs to maintain its current weight. The result will be a calorie deficit and an efficient and effective weight loss.

As I will show you, a diet that averages 400 calories per pound or lower can be extremely flexible, delicious, and varied—in fact, far more varied than you may realize. This diet is abundant in plant foods, especially vegetables, fruits, grains, and beans. It also contains a variety of animal foods. This diet will fill your stomach, create complete satisfaction, and yet provide you with a daily calorie deficit that will cause weight loss.

As you will see in Chapter 9, this diet not only will cause weight loss, but can also dramatically improve your health.

People sometimes ask me if this system works for different sizes of people. The answer is yes. First, stomach and body sizes are fairly proportional. Smaller people have smaller stomachs, which means they fill up on less food than bigger people. Bigger people have bigger stomachs, it's true, but the bigger you are, the more calories you need just to sustain normal metabolic function. That means, of course, that the bigger you are, the more calories you need to maintain your weight. By eating a diet below 400 calories per pound, small and large people will fill up their stomachs, yet not get enough calories to maintain their current weight. Which means they will lose weight.

MEALS BETWEEN 400 AND 600 CALORIES PER POUND MAINTAIN WEIGHT

If your meals average between 400 and 600 calories per pound, you're essentially at a break-even point. You will be able to eat until you are full and the calories you consume will be sufficient to maintain your current weight. You won't lose weight, but if you're active and exercising regularly, you will likely not gain weight, either. This is an important figure to shoot for when you travel or go out to eat. If you are losing weight, but want to enjoy a break from your diet, you want the meals you eat in restaurants to fall between 400 and 600 calories per pound.

600 TO 900 — ONLY FOR THE MOST ACTIVE YOUNG PEOPLE

Only extremely active young people who exercise rigorously each day will be able to maintain their weight at this calorie density. Everyone else will gain weight. In fact, if you are averaging a calorie density above 600 calories per pound, you are very likely eating many foods whose calorie density is far above 600 calories per pound. That's easy to do. Most of the processed foods—even bread—have calorie densities well above that figure (bread provides 1,280 calories per pound). These foods will drive up your average calorie density and promote weight gain. Also, people whose diets average more than 600 calories per pound are probably already overweight, even if they exercise.

ABOVE 900 CALORIES PER POUND

When your meals average 900 calories per pound, you are rapidly on your way to obesity. Nearly everyone gains weight at this average calorie density, even young, active men and women.

COMBINING FOODS TO KEEP YOUR CALORIE DENSITY BELOW 400

The way to keep the average calorie density of your meals low is to use the foods with a mid-range calorie density as the center of your meal, and then add low-calorie dense foods to bring down the average calorie density of your meal. Essentially, that means eating whole, unprocessed grains, beans, and low-fat animal foods, such as fish, as your main entrée, and then adding vegetables, nonfat dairy products, and fruit to bring down the meal's average calorie density.

For a minute, let's categorize different foods according to their varying levels, or tiers, of calorie density and see how you can combine them to bring down their average calorie densities.

The first and most effective tool for lowering the average calorie density of your meal is vegetables. Most vegetables fall below 200 calories per pound. Vegetables are going to bring down the average calorie density of every meal you eat.

Nonfat dairy products, including nonfat cottage cheese, yogurt, and ricotta cheese, fall within the range of 280 to 420, but most of the ones we recommend are below 300 calories per pound. They are the next most effective way of bringing down your average calorie density.

The high-carbohydrate foods, such as unprocessed grains, peas, and potatoes, along with pasta and hot cereals, range from 230 to 630 calories per pound. These can be considered the mid-range foods, the balance point, if you will. I recommend that you make these foods your main entrée, the meal's centerpiece. They are rich in nutrition and fiber, very filling, and highly satisfying. By adding vegetables to these mid-range foods, you easily can bring down the meal's average calorie density to well below 400 calories per pound.

While the caloric density of beans and lentils runs a little higher than other preferred carbohydrates, their very high-fiber content increases their satiety value—meaning they fill you up and keep you feeling full well after you've eaten your meal.

Fish can be found on the next tier up with calorie densities that start from about 400 per pound for orange roughy to the fatty fish, such as salmon, with a calorie density of 660 calories a pound. Most white fish are mid-range foods. As long as they are combined with lots of vegetables, a meal's average calorie density easily can be brought to below 400 calories per pound.

Chicken and meat represent the next level up. Chicken provides calorie densities anywhere from 750 (broiled breast without the skin) to 890 (with it) to 1,040 (the leg with the skin) to 1,190 (breaded, baked, or fried with the skin). McDonald's Chicken McNuggets provide 1,170 calories per pound. Meat ranges from a low of 780 calories per pound (ham) to as much as 2,150 (short ribs), 2,170 (bacon), and 2,260 (pepperoni). Extra lean ground beef provides about 1,130 calories per pound; porterhouse steak, 1,390; and pork chops, 1,560.

At this point, it's becoming difficult to bring down the average calorie density of a meal to below 400 calories per pound. However, if you combine the leanest forms of fish, chicken, or meat with plenty of vegetables, you can get your meal's average calorie density to below 400 calories per pound. In fact, this is what I recommend you do whenever you are in a restaurant—combine a moderate-calorie dense dish with foods that are low in calorie density, such as vegetables. In this way, you will be able to enjoy many moderate-calorie dense foods and still loose weight. (More on restaurant eating, party foods, and cheating in Chapter 3.)

The next level up, which consists mostly of dried carbohydrate-rich foods, takes you out of the weight loss and weight maintenance realms. Breads, bagels, dry cereals, baked chips, and crackers range from 1,150 to 1,750, and when consumed in large amounts virtually guarantee weight gain for most people. I recommend that if you are interested in losing weight, you should limit these foods. However, you can mitigate their weight-producing effects by eating them with lots of vegetables, or fruit, or some low-calorie dense dips.

Here are a couple of easy-to-follow rules that can keep your average calorie density below 400 calories per pound.

THE ONE-AND-ONE RULE

Every carbohydrate food should be accompanied by at least one vegetable. When you eat a baked potato or a portion of brown rice, add a vegetable dish, such as tomato, green beans, zucchini, broccoli, carrots, kale, asparagus, collard greens, onions, or spinach.

In most cases, vegetables only enhance the flavor and texture of food. A good example is pasta primavera, or noodles and marinara sauce with a variety of vegetables mixed in. Another example is a vegetable medley, sautéed in wine or chicken broth, over brown rice, some other grain, or mixed within a bean dish. Onions create a luscious, creamy texture that is wonderful with grains, while bell peppers sautéed in chicken broth or wine work perfectly when mixed with beans.

Be sure to prepare such entrées with little—and preferably no—oil or butter. The meal will still be delicious and satisfying and low in calorie density. If you order it at a restaurant, ask that the noodles and vegetables be prepared with the least amount of oil possible.

Keep in mind that all natural foods contain fat or its liquid form, which is oil. The abundance of grains and vegetables in the Pritikin Program will provide you with all the essential oils your body needs to be healthy.

Add a salad with balsamic vinegar and you've got a very low-calorie dense meal.

THE ONE-AND-TWO RULE

Every high-protein dish should be accompanied by two vegetables. Beans, seafood, poultry, or meat should never be eaten alone, because these foods are higher in calorie density. Lower the calorie density by adding two vegetables. For example, whenever you eat fish, or lentils, or black beans, add a salad—without an oily dressing—and steamed broccoli, or carrots and onions. You do not have to restrict yourself to two vegetables. If you eat a piece of cod, for example, have a salad and some other vegetable, such as asparagus or broccoli rabe. Add several vegetables and lower the calorie density even further. Surround your main entrée with vegetables. Not only will they contribute to weight loss, but they will boost your health dramatically.

MORE THAN MERE NUMBERS

All of this food combining is more than just a numbers game. The reason is that the more fiber and water you eat, the quicker your stomach will fill up, thus crowding out other high-calorie dense foods. By adding fibrous and water-rich foods, we are actually preventing you from consuming calories. A good example is adding sliced strawberries or some other fresh fruit to shredded wheat. A calorie-counting program would forbid you from adding strawberries to your shredded wheat because that program would view the fruit as a source of additional calories. Such programs apply the same rules to all foods, namely: eat less of everything, no matter what the food's calorie density is. In order to do that, you must control your appetite, which means you have to be hungry all the time.

With calorie density, we can distinguish between a food that has concentrated calories from those that are calorically light; by knowing the difference, we can minimize the high-calorie dense foods and maximize foods with low calorie density. But we are able to use another tool, which is to combine foods to lower their average calorie density.

The strawberries have a calorie density of about 140 calories per pound. The shredded wheat has a calorie density of about 1,610 calories per pound. When you average the two together, you've moved dramatically closer to our 400 calorie goal. Something else happens when you add strawberries to shredded wheat, however: They keep you from eating more shredded wheat. The strawberries create greater satisfaction and add pleasure to the food. But they also fill you up more quickly, which will keep you from going back for seconds and thirds of the dried cereal. Even more, the strawberries, like all fruit, provide many cancer-protective phytochemicals, as well as fiber, vitamins, and minerals that are important for your health.

Adding foods to lower the average calorie density is an important way of improving the enjoyment of your food and promoting more rapid and efficient weight loss.

THREE WAYS TO RECOGNIZE
CALORIE DENSITY—WITHOUT THE CHARTS

At this point, you may be convinced of the importance of calorie density, but worried that you may have to carry around a bunch of charts in order to distinguish low-calorie dense foods from high. That won't be necessary, because there's a simple way to determine a weight-producing food from a weight-loser.

There are three factors to keep in mind when determining calorie density: Water, fiber, and fat content. All three of these factors are controlled when you eat the preferred carbohydrates, namely unprocessed grains, vegetables, beans, and fruit.

1. WATER CONTENT DETERMINES CALORIE DENSITY

Water provides volume but no calories. If your stomach holds two or three pounds of food, and much of the weight of that food is created by water, than the number calories you've consumed will be substantially reduced. Water, in effect, dilutes a food's calorie content.

Processing, on the other hand, very often dries a food and concentrates its calories. Therefore, choose foods that contain water and avoid those that have been dried.

COOKED IN WATER TO LOWER CALORIE DENSITY

Foods cooked in water undergo a similar reduction in calorie content, because the food retains the water while in your stomach. One of the reasons whole, unprocessed grains and beans have a moderate calorie density is because they absorb much of the water in which they are cooked. The same goes for oatmeal and noodles, both processed, but both low in calorie density. Oatmeal contains about 280 calories per pound—a very low-calorie dense food.

Whole-wheat pasta has a moderate calorie density of 560 calories per pound, while white pasta provides 630 calories per pound. As I showed earlier in this chapter, if either form of pasta is combined with vegetables to make a pasta primavera, the calorie densities of these foods can be lowered to weight-reducing levels. It's worth noting, as well, that whole-wheat pasta contains fiber, which helps to keep you from getting hungry for a longer period of time.

Fat-free, sugar-free jello and puddings, both of which contain water but no fiber, are foods that have a low calorie density, and thus are good choices for weight loss.

WHEN IT COMES TO WEIGHT LOSS,
EATING WATER IS MORE EFFECTIVE THAN DRINKING IT

While calorie density is lowered when a food is cooked in water, it is not lowered when you simply drink water while eating a dry, processed food. Processed foods that are cooked in water retain their water content, which means they are bulkier and have greater volume. They're going to fill you up on fewer calories.

But processed foods that are dry when eaten—even if you drink water with them—don't bulk up because of the water. In fact, the water, which is not part of the food, tends to be rapidly absorbed into the bloodstream, leaving behind the calorie dense food you've eaten. For example, if you eat chips and drink water, the water will be taken into your blood, but the chips, with all their calories, will be digested and absorbed separately. The same thing happens when you eat dried cereals with milk. The liquid, which isn't bound by the cereal, is quickly absorbed, while the processed food, and all its calories, is treated separately. This is why the old trick of drinking lots of water to help you feel full on a portion-controlled diet never really worked.

Interestingly, water tends to increase our capacity for eating dry, calorie dense foods. Your body demands that you drink water in order to keep eating potato chips, for example. And you couldn't eat a lot of dried fruit unless you drank water, as well.

When water is contained within food, as it is with fresh fruit, you do not feel compelled to drink water while eating your food. The food itself provides all the water your body needs in order to enjoy the particular fruit or vegetable.

2. FIBER DISPLACES CALORIES

Fiber offers an array of benefits when it comes to calorie density. For one thing, it holds water, which contributes to its ability to add bulk and thus create feelings of fullness. Fiber also slows the time it takes for your stomach to empty.

By remaining in your stomach longer, fiber prolongs your feelings of being full long after your meal has been consumed. Choose foods that contain fiber over those that do not, even when the calorie densities are relatively the same. As much as possible, choose beans over chicken, brown rice over white rice, and whole-wheat pasta over white pasta.

Fiber provides many health benefits, but it also helps lower the calorie density of your meals.

When comparing water and fiber, water is clearly more important in determining a food's calorie density. Vegetables and fruits are loaded with both, which is why they are so low in calories.

STAY AWAY FROM DRY AND CRISPY

Dry and crispy foods are very likely to be high in calorie density and therefore will promote weight gain. That includes many seemingly innocuous foods, such as dried fruit. Fresh fruit, which contains both water and fiber, is very low in caloric density at 140 to 420 calories per pound. But dry that fruit and concentrate the calories and now you've got a food that ranges between 1,080 and 1,470 calories per pound.

Another way to think of the caloric density of fresh fruit versus dried is to ask yourself whether you could ever eat as much fresh fruit as you could dried. People can down a dozen or more dried apricots or dried pear slices, but those same people couldn't eat nearly as many whole apricots or whole pears.

Another good example is whole-wheat bread. Dried during processing, bread contains about 1,280 calories per pound. On the other hand, whole-wheat pasta—also a wheat product, but one that is cooked in water—has a calorie density of about 560 calories per pound.

As we've already seen, popcorn, also dry and crispy, contains 1,730 calories per pound. Here are some more examples:

- Snackwell's Cookie Cakes   1,420 cal./lb.

- Dry cereals   1,130 to 2,210 cal./lb.

- Fat-free baked chips   1,760 cal./lb.

Any food that is dried in processing has had its calories concentrated. If the fiber has been removed, the calories have been concentrated all the more.

3. ADD FAT AND WATCH THE CALORIE DENSITY SKYROCKET

Animal foods present a more complex picture when seen through the calorie density lens. Some animal foods are relatively low in calorie density, others relatively high, depending on their fat content. The water in fish, chicken, and beef brings their calorie density down, but the fat content, when it is high, more than offsets the reduction in calorie density provided by the water.

Naturally, the higher the fat content, the higher the calorie density. Chicken breast, which is lower in fat than sirloin steak, has a lower calorie density (750 versus 870, respectively). Shellfish, which is lower in fat than many fish, provides as little as 460 calories per pound; cod, halibut, and orange roughy are right around 400 calories per pound, while salmon, a high-fat fish, contains 700 to 800 calories per pound. As fat content goes up, calorie density rises as well.

DOUBLE TROUBLE

The fastest road to overweight and obesity is to add fat to foods whose calories have been dried and concentrated. Full-fat potato chips, chocolate chip cookies, granola, and French fries are double trouble. Here are the numbers:

- French fries   1,450

- Trail mix   2,100

- M & Ms   2,270

- Granola bar, hard   2,140

- Granola cereal   2,210

- Butter and margarine   3,250

- Fats and oils   3,250 to 4,000 +

THE PRITIKIN PROGRAM: LOW CALORIE DENSITY, HIGH NUTRITION

Most of the foods on the Pritikin Program are very low in calorie density. Consequently, they cause ongoing weight loss. We are not only concerned about weight, however, but also with health. Therefore, we teach you how to use the calorie density principle to lower weight, as well as prevent and overcome disease.

The Pritikin Eating Plan is made up largely of plant foods; it also includes up to three and a half ounces of animal foods and two servings of non fat milk products per day. We recommend that fish, chicken, and meat be eaten as a condiment—that is as small pieces with lots of vegetables. If the day's allotment of three and a half ounces of animal food is eaten at a single meal, then the rest of the day's meals should consist entirely of plant foods. We recommend restricting animal food not so much for their respective calorie densities, but for their saturated fat and cholesterol content. Many animal foods are low in calorie density—some fish, lobster, and game meat, for example—but all contain some saturated fat and cholesterol, and many provide significant amounts of these substances. Therefore, we restrict these foods for their effects on health, rather than on weight.

The calorie density chart on page 34 shows the recommended foods on the Pritikin Program. Following the chart is a list of some of the foods that are included in the program. Chapter 5 provides a much fuller description of the Pritikin Eating Plan; it also provides menus for seven days' worth of breakfasts, lunches, dinners, snacks, and desserts. Chapter 6 provides the calorie density for these and many other commonly consumed foods, snacks, and desserts.

When creating your meals, always keep the Pritikin Principles in mind: Eat the preferred carbohydrate foods, which, in most cases, are whole, unprocessed grains, vegetables, beans, and fruit; and eat foods low in fat, cholesterol, and salt.

FOODS TO EAT ON PRITIKIN PROGRAM

FOOD	CALORIES PER POUND (range)

NATURAL AND MINIMALLY PROCESSED FOODS

Vegetables	60 to 215
Fruits	140 to 420
Most nonfat dairy products (nonfat cheeses are higher)	160 to 450
Potatoes, yams, brown rice, pasta, hot cereals	240 to 630
Beans, peas, lentils (cooked)	310 to 780
Game meat (venison, rabbit)	600 to 860
Fish, chicken, turkey (skinless white meat), shellfish	400 to 750

THE PRITIKIN DIET: THE BIG PICTURE

The Pritikin Eating Plan, which now includes the calorie density principle, is composed primarily of whole, unprocessed plant foods that are rich in carbohydrates, fiber, and other nutrients. The eating plan also includes low-fat animal foods and an endless variety of soups, spices, herbs, sauces, and dressings. Among the foods included in the plan are:

VEGETABLES

Included in the wide assortment of vegetables on the diet are: asparagus, broccoli, Brussels sprouts, carrots, celery, Chinese cabbage, collard greens, cucumber, endive, escarole, green beans, ginger, kale, leeks, lettuce, mushrooms, mustard greens, okra, onion, radish, rutabaga, tomato, turnip, watercress, zucchini.

BEANS

Including: azuki beans, black beans, black-eyed peas, chickpeas, Great Northern beans, kidney beans, lima beans, lentils, navy beans, pinto beans, soybeans, and all peas (fresh and dried). Also bean products such as tofu and tempeh, soybean products loaded with protective phytochemicals, including phytoestrogens.

FRUIT

Such as apples, bananas, blackberries, blueberries, grapefruit, mangoes, oranges, papaya, pears, plums, and strawberries.

WHOLE GRAINS AND CARBOHYDRATE-RICH FOODS

The recommended grains are: brown rice, barley, buckwheat, corn, millet, oats, rye, wheat (including bulgur and whole-wheat berries), and whole-grain hot cereals. We also include all forms of pasta, especially whole-wheat pasta, potatoes, sweet potatoes, and yams.

LOW-FAT ANIMAL FOODS

Note: We recommend that low-fat animal foods are eaten only once a day and that the portions are limited to 3½ ounces per day. The low-fat animal foods we recommend include: fish, the white meat of chicken and turkey without the skin, lean beef (select grade), egg whites, and nonfat cheeses. We limit the amounts of these foods because we are concerned about their cholesterol and saturated fat content, both of which drive up blood cholesterol and are associated with higher levels of heart disease, cancer, and other degenerative illnesses.

NONFAT MILK PRODUCTS

The program includes 2 servings of nonfat dairy products, such as 1 cup of skim milk; ¾-cup-servings of nonfat yogurt; or 2 ounces per serving of nonfat cheese, or ½ cup of nonfat ricotta cheese.

HERBS AND SPICES

A wide variety of herbs and spices are provided in our recipes, which you'll find in Chapter 10.

FOODS TO MINIMIZE OR AVOID

In general, you will want to avoid foods that have been highly refined or processed and those that contain significant amounts of fat. They are sources of concentrated calories, as well as saturated fat, which causes heart disease, adult-onset diabetes, cancer, and overweight.

In the next chapter, I will show you how you can include small amounts of highly desirable foods, such as olive oil, avocado (used for making guacamole), and other tasty foods and condiments that may be higher in fat or calorie density.

For people who are lean and not concerned about their weight, some healthful sources of concentrated calories, such as whole-grain bread and whole-grain rolls, do not have to be avoided. In fact, these foods are rich in fiber and other nutrients and can be part of a healthful diet. But for those concerned about weight, these foods can prevent weight loss and add pounds.

The following foods should be avoided by anyone who is interested in efficient and effective weight loss. Many of these processed foods are very high in calorie density. Others are rich in fat, which is the most calorically dense substance in the food supply.

Let's look at the foods you will want to minimize or avoid in order to achieve optimal weight.

FOODS TO MINIMIZE OR AVOID

FOOD	CALORIES PER POUND (range)
CALORIE DENSE PROCESSED FOODS WITH LITTLE OR NO FAT	
Breads, bagels, fat-free muffins	920 to 1,360
Dry cereals, baked chips, fat-free crackers, pretzels	1,480 to 1,910
Sugar	1,730
HIGH -FAT FOODS	
Avocado	800
French fries	1,400 to 1,500
Cheese, sausages, bologna, bacon	1,270 to 2,300
Chocolate bars, croissants, cookies, donuts, granola bars, pastries	1,190 to 2,780
Potato chips, corn chips, Pringles, nuts, seeds	2,400 to 3,260
Meats	820 to 2,260
Fats and oils	3,200 to 4,100

By following the recommended Pritikin Eating Plan, you will easily keep the average calorie density of your meals below 400 calories per pound. As long as you are walking daily, the eating plan will help you lose your excess weight without being hungry, cold, or tired.

Now that you know the basic rules for the Calorie Density Principle, let's look at ways to bend them a little to enhance your enjoyment of the Pritikin Eating Plan—while you are losing weight. That's in the next chapter. But before we get to that, here's another Pritikin success story.

DOROTHY'S STORY

Optimal weight has proven so difficult for people to achieve and sustain that it's perfectly understandable why so many people question if such a thing is even possible.

That was the case with Dorothy, who in 1996, at the age of 60, suffered from adult-onset diabetes, high blood pressure, arrhythmias, and obesity. She was more than 100 pounds overweight. She could manage only a few steps before she was out of breath and looking for support, either from her walker or from someone nearby.

Dorothy had been the overweight child of overweight parents and spent most of her life struggling with her weight and its effects on her self-esteem. She had tried every diet and weight loss program that appeared on the market, it seemed. Any weight she lost initially was always followed by relapse and additional weight gain. Most people at Dorothy's age would have given up, but for reasons even she doesn't understand, she persevered and continued to believe that a better life lay ahead.

"It all paid off," she said recently, "when I found the Pritikin Program."

One of the problems Dorothy encountered during her many years of dieting was that her health worsened whenever she adopted a new program. This was especially the case when she adopted a high-protein, high-fat regimen. "I couldn't stay on these diets because my heart and diabetes got worse," she said.

In 1996, a friend told her about the Pritikin Longevity Center and urged Dorothy to visit the Center and try the program. "A little bell rang in my head when I heard my friend's words and after thinking about it for awhile, and finding out more about Pritikin, I decided to go for a month."

As if to add insult and incentive to her quest, Dorothy needed a seat belt extender on her flight to the Center. She had great difficulty getting in and out of her airline seat.

The transformation of Dorothy Durand is so great that even she cannot believe such changes were ever possible. Today, Dorothy is 130 pounds lighter. She has the energy of someone decades younger. She takes no insulin or medication for her diabetes and is symptom free; her blood pressure is normal and she suffers from no heart arrhythmias. On the contrary, she walks, stretches, and does flex exercises daily; twice a week she does low-impact aerobics and once a week she even attends ballroom dancing classes. "My life has changed in every way," she said recently. "After all these years, I've just started to live."

3 | HOW TO CHEAT AND STILL LOSE WEIGHT

What's the fun of being on a diet if you can't cheat occasionally? Discipline, if taken too far, can become a kind of prison. The problem with cheating on any diet, as we all know, is that it can be like pulling your finger out of the dike. It lets loose a flood of behaviors that amount to, well, being off your diet and gaining weight. Intuitively, we all know that cheating is often the first step to failure. It's the crack in the wall, the breaking of your will's main support beam. Pretty soon, the dike is collapsing and all of your good intentions and the lofty goals are rushing away from you—and with them any hope of becoming the best version of yourself. Perhaps that's why failure on any self-help program hurts a little more than we might have expected.

My point in saying all of this is to illustrate how paradoxical cheating can be. On one hand, it's essential that you relax occasionally, assuming, of course, that your health permits a small deviation from time to time. (I have a lot more to say about health and how to use the Pritikin Program to overcome serious illnesses in Chapters 8 and 9.) Such digressions can actually strengthen and renew your commitment to all of your goals. But cheating can also be like dancing on the edge of a slippery slope. One wrong move, one chip and dip too many, and, whoa! Before you know it, you're a year down the road and 20 pounds heavier.

There are two ways to keep from making this mistake. The first is to know how to cheat. The second is to do the right thing after cheating—at the next meal, or during the following day. On this program, doing the right thing means eating foods that are low in calorie density to compensate for the previous day's high-calorie dense meals, and doing a little extra exercise.

In this chapter, I want to teach you how to cheat and, at the same time, stay on track so that you can realize every goal you have established for yourself on the Pritikin Program.

WHEN IT COMES TO CHEATING, TIMING MATTERS

The calorie density principle teaches you how to fill up your stomach on foods that will provide you with relatively few calories. The principle, by itself, can cause you to lose the excess body fat that threatens your health and longevity. One of the ways to ensure that you keep the average calorie density of your meals low is by employing a strategy I call "sequencing."

The idea, essentially, is this: During any single meal, eat the foods with the lowest calorie density first and then eat in sequence from the lowest calorie density to the relatively highest. In effect, you are choosing to eat foods in a specific order—starting out with the food that has the lowest-calorie density and the greatest satiety value and then proceeding to the next highest. By choosing the lowest calorie-dense foods first, you will be eating the foods that will take up the most room in your stomach, while providing the fewest calories. In a kind of stairway fashion, you will be moving upward in calorie density, but at the same time filling your stomach, so that there's less and less room for foods with the higher calorie densities. Always save the relatively higher-calorie dense foods for the end of the meal. By that time, you'll be full and there won't be much room left in your stomach to eat very much of those foods. You will be perfectly happy to eat less of that food, and yet you will enjoy that food immensely.

This strategy should be used for any meal—that is, when you are eating foods that are acceptable, but still relatively high in calorie density, or when you are cheating. Whatever situation you are finding yourself in, eat the higher-calorie dense foods at the end of the meal, after you have filled up on foods with lower calorie density.

Start out your meal with a salad with nonfat dressing, such as balsamic vinegar, and, if possible, a vegetable-based soup, for example. Both of these foods are very low in calorie density. They will take the edge off your hunger and leave less room in your stomach for the other foods. Whatever else is on your plate, eat more of the calorically light foods and less of the calorically dense. In this way, you can enjoy the foods that are moderately high in calorie density, while you fill up on high-satiety, calorically light foods.

Many traditional cultures, especially the Chinese, employ this strategy by including more calorically light foods—such as vegetables and rice—in combination with foods that have higher calorie density. This provides the enjoyment of having the animal food as part of your meal, but lowers its calorie density by including lots of low-calorie dense foods with it. When used in either way, the animal food entrée need not be a large portion. We recommend that such servings of animal foods only be 3½ ounces, which is ample, given that you have already filled your stomach with low-calorie dense foods.

By following this pattern, you will have created a calorie deficit— meaning you will be taking in fewer calories than you burn each day. That is the basis for weight loss.

You can also use sequencing to give you greater freedom to enjoy foods that may be higher in calorie density than you normally would eat. As long as you consistently keep the average calorie density of your meals low—an average of 400 calories per pound or lower—you will have created a substantial calorie deficit. That deficit could be so large, in fact, that you will have some freedom to eat a higher-calorie dense food at the end of one of these meals—say a dessert you especially like—and still lose weight.

The net effect of sequencing is to create satiety, satisfaction, and a calorie deficit—in short, to lose weight without ever being hungry or feeling deprived.

TED'S LOVE OF PIZZA

As I was teaching the calorie density principle one day at the Pritikin Longevity Center, one of our participants, a man named Ted, told me that he loved pizza and didn't think he could give it up. "There must be some way I can use this principle to allow myself a little pizza now and then and still lose weight," he told me.

"There is," I said. "The first thing you have to think of whenever you're about to eat a high-calorie dense food is to fill your stomach with foods that are low in calorie density first. In essence, we want to provide as little room for the calorically dense foods as we can. There's lots of ways you can reduce the calorie density of a pizza binge. First, before you eat that pizza, eat a big salad and, if possible, a small bowl of pasta that contains vegetables. Have lots of vegetables on the pizza itself and, if you can, order a cheeseless pizza. When you get the pizza, split it among the people you're with. And be sure to stay away from the pepperoni."

EAT YOUR CALORIES—DON'T DRINK THEM

The greater your daily calorie deficit, the more freedom you will have on the Pritikin Program, assuming once again that your overall health permits such freedom. Unfortunately, there are so many hidden calories in the standard American diet that it's often difficult to create that deficit, even when we seem to be doing everything right. A major source of additional calories that few people think about is the beverages we drink.

Solids and liquids have very different effects on the stomach and your hunger. Once consumed, solid foods stretch the stomach and trigger your satiety receptors—the nerves in your stomach that tell your brain that your stomach is full—thus keeping you from eating any more food. Solid foods can linger in your stomach sometimes for hours, depending on the kind of food you eat. In this way, they have a kind of ongoing satiety value. Liquids stretch the stomach initially, as well, but they quickly empty into the small intestine and then are absorbed into the bloodstream. This rapid emptying of the stomach gives only a short-term sense of fullness, which means that no matter how many calories you consumed in liquid form, you are soon hungry again. As you probably know, soda, fruit juice, and alcoholic beverages provide significant numbers of calories.

After reviewing 40 studies on the influence of solids and liquids on satiety, Purdue University researcher Richard Mattes found that when people overeat solid foods at a particular meal, they compensate for the additional calories by eating less throughout the rest of the day. Mattes told the *Nutrition Action Healthletter* (April 1999) that, "if you gave people 100 extra calories as solid food, they would compensate by consuming 67 fewer calories during the rest of the day, so only 33 calories would be surplus." By which he means that only 33 calories go toward increasing your weight.

On the other hand, "if you fed them 100 calories in a soda, juice or other clear liquid, they wouldn't reduce their intake at all. All 100 calories would be surplus."

Interestingly, semisolid foods, such as gelatins and milkshakes, remain inside the stomach longer than liquids do, but not as long as solids. "If you gave [people] 100 calories in semisolid foods," Mattes told *Nutrition Action*, "they would only reduce their intake by about 20 calories, so 80 would be surplus." That means, of course, that semisolid foods with little or no fiber are almost as bad at increasing weight as liquids.

The following chart illustrates how solids, semisolids, and liquids affect our calorie consumption.

FOOD TYPE	NUMBER OF EXTRA CALORIES	NUMBER OF SURPLUS CALORIES RETAINED, IF ANY	FEWER CALORIES CONSUMED THE REST OF THE DAY
Solid food	100 additional calories	33 calories	67
Semisolid	100 additional calories	80 calories	20
Liquid Beverage	100 additional calories	100 calories	0

As I have been saying, we must create satiety on relatively few calories if we are to be successful at losing weight. A healthy weight can only be achieved, and maintained, when you are full and satisfied with your diet. High-calorie liquids work against us because they add calories but still leave us hungry for solid foods, which only add even more calories. Thus, the more calories we consume as liquids, the more weight we will add to our bodies. Therefore, if you want to lose weight, drink beverages that provide few if any calories. Spring and tap water, of course, provide none. Soups that contain vegetables, whole grains, and/or beans are an excellent weight loss food because they still have plenty of fiber to delay stomach emptying and prolong satiety after the meal is finished.

Interestingly, the elderly could put such mechanics to good use. Many elderly people have trouble putting weight on and keeping it on. They could supplement their diets with high-calorie liquids, which would not affect their appetite, but would increase their calorie intake.

FREEDOM THROUGH ADDITION: OR HOW TO CHEAT ON CHIPS AND GUACAMOLE AND STILL LOSE WEIGHT

When we use the calorie density principle, we must always be thinking about adding foods to our meals. This program emphasizes the addition of foods low in calorie density, rather than simply by subtracting high-calorie dense foods. You might think this is just semantics, but it's not true. When you emphasize adding low-calorie dense foods, you are creating satiety, or fullness. When you emphasize subtracting foods, you are secretly creating hunger and feelings of deprivation and thus setting yourself up for failure.

Adding foods is one of the keys to safe and effective cheating. Remember that we must always be thinking of ways to bring down the average

43

calorie density of our meals. We can do this by adding a lower-calorie dense food to a meal or snack. The food with the lower calorie density will bring down the average calorie density of the meal, or snack, and thus mitigate its weight-producing effects. Take chips and guacamole, for example.

Tortilla corn chips provide about 2,400 calories per pound. Guacamole is made from the high-fat fruit, avocados, which provide 800 calories per pound. However, when avocados are mixed with tomatoes and other salsa ingredients to make guacamole, the condiment falls to about 480 calories per pound. Unlike the chips, guacamole contains water and fiber, which is a major reason why it has a lower calorie density than the chips. Let's say that you're at a party and you're hungry. In fact, let's say you're so hungry that you could eat a standard size bag of chips, which contains a full pound, or 2,400 calories. Oh, no! you say. You're hungry and your will power is caving in. What can you do? Simple: Add a lower-calorie dense food to the chips, which will bring down the average calorie density of your snack. Enter the guacamole—or should I say, guacamole to the rescue?

Remember our fish bowl metaphor in Chapter 2. Let's say that instead of eating a pound of chips, you eat half a pound. And instead of eating a pound of guacamole, you eat half a pound. When the calorie densities of those two foods are combined, you get a snack with a calorie density of 1,440 calories per pound. Because you did in fact eat a pound of food, you actually ate 1,440 calories, but you've lowered that calorie density to 960 calories by adding guacamole, which made the snack a lot more satisfying and filling than the chips would have been alone. (The math works like this: To arrive at the average calorie density between these two foods, you add 2,400 calories per pound for the chips, plus 480 calories per pound for the dip, and arrive at 2,880 calories per pound. That number is divided by two—there are two foods—to get 1,440 calories per pound.)

By combining a high-calorie dense food with one that is lower in caloric density, you have actually lowered the number of calories you have consumed, even though you did it by adding a food that is high in fat. You can further reduce the calorie density of the snack described above by adding lots of chopped tomato and onion to the guacamole.

Interestingly, by adding guacamole to chips, you have also reduced your consumption of hydrogenated (or partially saturated) fat, which is present in the chips, and substituted monounsaturated fat from the guacamole. In the process, you've had a less harmful effect on your heart. Hydrogenated fat raises blood cholesterol and contributes to heart disease, stroke, and cancer. Monounsaturated fat has only a small effect on blood cholesterol.

In fact, most people find chips and guacamole a lot more satisfying—

and more filling—than chips alone. The chips and guacamole are still a weight-producing combination, but when you're socializing with friends, you want to let your hair down. With the calorie density principle as your guide, you can do exactly that and still keep your waistline in check.

You can use the calorie density principle to bring down the calories even further by eating fat-free baked chips, which provide only 1,920 calories per pound. My wife loves chips and whenever she reaches for a handful of chips, I tell her, with tongue in cheek, "You cannot have those chips—unless, you eat bean dip with them." When she complies, I tell her that, "You cannot have that bean dip—unless you combine it with salsa." The salsa brings the bean dip down to around 400 calories a pound, which is well within the healthy snack range for someone who eats vegetables at every meal and exercises daily.

A LITTLE OLIVE OIL CAN BE PART OF A LOW-CALORIE DENSE MEAL

One of the more confusing subjects within nutrition today is the Mediterranean diet and specifically the use of olive oil. Today we are hearing so much about olive oil that you would think it's the next panacea for everything that ails us. Don't believe it. For all its positive attributes, olive oil is still a liquid fat that provides about 4,000 calories per pound. It will add pounds to your body as quickly as hamburgers and French fries—in fact, it will do it even faster, because both of those foods have lower calorie densities than olive oil. On the other hand, olive oil is primarily a monounsaturated fat. It has a minimal effect on your cholesterol level and may raise your levels of HDL cholesterol, the good cholesterol that provides some protection against heart disease. In addition to its positive benefits is its taste. Many people who are attempting to lose weight often feel deprived if they can't enjoy a little olive oil from time to time. So let me show you how you can have some olive oil and still keep the weight off.

Recently, I visited Greece and some of the Greek Islands and saw, once again, how slender many European people are. One of the paradoxes among Europeans—especially among Mediterranean people—is that they are leaner than Americans, but they eat olive oil. Researchers have been noting this same phenomenon for much of the decade and have drawn numerous conclusions from it, not all of them correct. Among the things I noticed when I observed Mediterranean people was that, first, many of them live on diets that, overall, are low in calorie density. That's how they stay so thin. They rely very heavily on vegetables and pasta as their staple foods. (Unfortunately, many keep the calorie intake down by being heavy cigarette smokers. Instead of eating, they light up a cigarette.)

A second observation I made was the way in which they use olive oil. Rather than spreading it on bread, which is how many Americans use olive oil today, Europeans add olive oil to vegetables. This, of course, brings down its calorie density dramatically and consequently has a very different effect on weight. If you use olive oil at all, you have to do the same thing.

At 4,000 calories per pound, fats are almost off the scale when it comes to calorie density. A tablespoon contains 125 calories. As we have been doing, the way we lower the calorie density of a meal is to combine fat with a food that has a lower calorie density. When it comes to mitigating the weight-producing effects of olive oil, we must combine it with a food with a low calorie density, namely vegetables.

Let's say that you use two tablespoons of olive oil (250 calories) on a pound of salad (which contains 100 calories), which is usually enough salad for four people. That amounts to a calorie density of 350 calories per pound for each person eating the salad—about the same calorie density of a boiled potato and well within our limits for weight loss. It still won't cause you to gain weight. (Here's how the math is done, if you are interested. The olive oil provides 4,000 calories per pound. Two tablespoons equal $\frac{1}{16}$ of a pound. By multiplying 4,000 calories per pound by $\frac{1}{16}$, the amount of olive oil actually consumed, you get 250 calories.)

As I tell people in my classes at the Pritikin Longevity Center, I would rather that people who are concerned about weight not eat olive oil. But many people have told me that they will not eat salads unless they sprinkle on some olive oil. Vegetables are essential to health and weight loss. They contain an abundance of vitamins, minerals, and other immune-boosting and cancer-fighting nutrients. They are low in calorie density. You have to eat vegetables if you expect to lose weight and feel good while you do it. Therefore, if the only way to get people to eat vegetables is to eat some small amounts of olive oil, I tell people to take the smallest portion of olive oil and use it only on vegetables.

Never add olive oil to bread, at least if you would like to lose weight. Bread, which is processed and dry, has a calorie density of around 1,280 calories per pound. It will put on pounds without the olive oil. But by sponging up the olive oil, with 4,000 calories per pound, it now becomes even more calorically dense than cheesecake. If you went out to dinner with someone trying to lose weight, and he or she ate bread with olive oil, you wouldn't blink an eye. But if you went out to eat with that same person and he or she ate cheesecake before the meal, you'd think they were a little bit strange—especially if they wanted to lose weight.

EAT FREQUENTLY AND LOSE WEIGHT

The principle of eating frequently and our efforts at calorie deficit are inextricably joined. As long as you eat a diet made up largely of low-calorie dense foods, you create an ongoing calorie deficit. In other words, you'll be eating an insufficient number of calories to maintain your present weight. That's going to do two things. First, it's going to require that your body burn its calorie reserves, which are tied up in your tissues as fat. Second, it's going to produce hunger. We do not want you to be hungry—it's the primary reason why people fail on weight loss programs—which means you'll have to eat frequently in order to avoid hunger.

On the Pritikin Program, we encourage you to eat three, low-calorie dense meals per day, along with two or three snacks—also low in calorie density—between meals. Eating frequently provides many benefits, the first of which is that it keeps you from being hungry.

Researchers have deduced that our early ancestors ate as many as eight to 12 times per day, and that most of their foods were plants. We evolved on a behavior pattern that is very different from our modern custom, which is to eat only two or three meals per day. Our ancestors had to eat frequently because they relied on foods that were very low in calorie density. Since each of their meals offered them only enough calories to support their activities for a few hours, or a day, they were driven to eat as many meals as they could. Early humans were continually experiencing what you and I know as the effects of a meal at a Chinese restaurant, the illustration I used in Chapter 1.

Chinese food fills your stomach, but because Chinese dishes are loaded with water and fiber, they are low in calorie density and ideal for weight loss. However, because they fill you up on very few calories, they also cause hunger two hours later. Low-calorie dense meals actually force you to eat frequently, because they are providing you with only enough calories to support your activity—and not enough to support your weight.

By doing this, you'll be avoiding hunger as you lose weight. Of course, most modern Americans do just the opposite every day. Many of us skip breakfast, or simply have a cup of coffee, which means we eat only two meals each day. The effect of infrequent eating is exactly the opposite of what many of us expect. Rather than reducing our calorie intake, infrequent eating triggers our innate "famine response," a biological urge that directs us to compensate for the lack of food by overeating, especially foods that are high in calories. Those who eat two or three meals per day are often driven to eat bigger, more calorie dense meals so they can take in as many calories as possible. This is why infrequent eating—that is, eating two or three meals per day—often results in weight gain.

Frequent eating, on the other hand, keeps us from being hungry and triggering our famine response, which in turn allows us to maintain a low-calorie dense diet. That low-calorie dense diet creates and maintains a calorie deficit, which is the basis for weight loss.

Now, I know what those of you who have counted calories before are probably thinking: What if I eat one or two big meals and stay full for many hours—won't that provide me with just as many calories, in total, as the many low-calorie dense meals I eat throughout the day? The answer is no. Eating three low-calorie dense meals, along with two low-calorie dense snacks, will provide you with fewer calories overall than the two high-calorie dense meals—not to mention whatever snacks you eat with those high-calorie dense meals.

As long as your meals and snacks are low in calorie density, you will continue to keep your total calorie intake low, even as you eat every few hours and avoid hunger.

WHAT TO DO WHEN YOU RELAPSE

One of the beauties of the calorie density principle is that you know how to create a calorie deficit without hunger. If you have strayed too far from your program, you should immediately go back to the menus and recommended snacks provided in Chapter 5. That will rapidly bring the average calorie density of your diet down; you will immediately start to create a calorie deficit again. You can do this in a single day, which immediately gets you back on track and losing weight.

BILL'S STORY

Bill Winthrop, now 30, weighed 316 pounds when he decided to adopt the Pritikin Program back in 1995. Before that, "I was eating out for breakfast, lunch and dinner," he recalled recently. As with so many other people, overweight was only one of Bill's problems. He was continually tired, run down, and anxious. "I felt terrible," he recalled.

Even worse, Bill could see the future. All he had to do was look at his father, who was also overweight, suffered from adult-onset diabetes, and had had his first coronary bypass surgery at the age 47. "My Dad knew where I was headed," Bill said. "He'd show me his bypass scars and say, 'Do you want to go through this?'" The answer was no.

When Bill came to the Longevity Center and described his diet and lifestyle to me, I asked him what he ate each day. "I'm dieting all the time," he told me. And the truth was, Bill really was attempting to minimize the number of calories he ate each day. He just wasn't doing it effectively.

Each morning, Bill drank a cup of coffee and ate as light a lunch as he could manage, usually a sandwich with luncheon meat or tuna salad and a Coca-Cola. He did not eat anything between lunch and dinner; by dinner-time, he was starving. At that point, there was no holding his appetite back. Every night, he ate a large dinner, full of calorically rich foods, and didn't stop eating until an hour or so before he went to bed. The next morning, the cycle would start all over again. Obviously, because he went to bed with a full stomach, he wasn't very hungry in the morning, so a cup of coffee was all he wanted. But as the day progressed and his hunger started to build, he was constantly attempting to hold back his food intake—that is, until the dam broke every night. At that point, Bill's will power caved in and he ate until he was fully sated. Unfortunately, he satisfied his hunger on foods with very high calorie density.

If you looked at Bill's daily eating patterns, you would see that most of his calorie intake occurred every night after 5 p.m. He limited his food con-sumption during the morning and afternoon, but without realizing it, he habitually triggered his famine response. By the time the evening rolled around, he had absolutely no will power to control his eating habits. He was ravenous and, naturally, he gorged on high-calorie dense foods virtual-ly every night. In the end, his eating pattern was one of the main reasons he was so overweight.

One of the first things I told Bill was that he had to stop fasting during the morning and afternoon. Instead, he had to eat three meals, beginning with a filling breakfast composed of low-calorie dense foods, and two or three low-calorie dense snacks every day. At night, he should have a dinner composed of lots of low-calorie dense foods and then have a light snack in the evening. In essence, I wanted him to keep his hunger—and his famine response—at bay, while he filled up on foods that were low in calorie den-sity, but high in satiety value.

In order to keep himself full and satisfied, Bill had to learn to sequence his foods, as well. He had to fill up on the lowest-calorie dense foods at the start of the meal and then eat the foods with the higher calorie density after he was already partially sated. This allowed him to crowd out most of the calorie dense foods he was used to eating. It kept his famine response from controlling his eating pattern and also gave him the freedom to enjoy small-er portions of calorie dense foods.

Within weeks of adopting the program, Bill lost 20 pounds; his choles-terol level fell from 267 mg/dl to 200, and his triglycerides dropped from 656 to 232. He was on his way and he knew it.

Today, Bill weighs 195 pounds and at six feet two inches is lean and healthy. His cholesterol level is 145 mg/dl, well within the healthiest of ranges, and his triglycerides are 75. The numbers only tell part of the story. In fact, Bill is more active than even he ever dreamed possible. He hikes, bikes, backpacks, and skydives. "It's amazing how much I've changed," Bill said recently. "I always wanted to do these things, but I used to get so tired so quickly. . . . I can remember calling up places and being told, 'You're too heavy.' . . . It seemed there was always a weight limit and I was beyond it." Not anymore.

4 | WHY DIETS DON'T WORK (AND WHY THIS ONE WILL)

Why do diets fail? That's a question more people should be asking. The reason it's not asked as much as it should be is because most dieters think they already know the answer. Ask people why their programs fail and they will tell you some version of the following: "Diets fail for me because I fail. At some point, my discipline breaks down, or I start craving certain foods. Pretty soon, I can't keep myself from eating foods that take me off the diet. That's when I regain all the weight I lost. In some cases, I end up being heavier than when I started dieting."

Sometimes the belief that we know something prevents us from learning the real truth. Most people do not fail on their diets. Actually, the reverse is true: Most diets fail them! The vast majority of diets today are impossible to maintain. Many create feelings of hunger and deprivation, which in turn trigger cravings for calorie dense foods. Eventually, those cravings must be satisfied. Once that happens, you're off the diet. The pressure on people today to lose weight is enormous. Thus, even when diets fail, we quickly take up another one in the hopes that this new program will work for us. Rather than repeating the same series of mistakes, let's look at why diets fail, and how we can succeed on a weight-reducing, health-enhancing program.

FOUR LITTLE SECRETS

There are a lot of weight loss programs out there—or so it seems. In fact, the market today seems flooded with them. Not surprisingly, each one claims to offer a unique approach to losing weight. Consequently, each trumpets itself as a new and revolutionary answer to an old and intractable problem. But are there really that many weight loss programs, or are there only a few basic diets that entrepreneurs dress up to make them appear different from the others? Here are four little secrets of the weight loss industry that most people don't realize.

First, every diet program uses the same principle to cause weight loss, which is this: Weight loss is accomplished by consuming fewer calories than you burn each day as fuel. No matter what kind of program you adopt—whether it's a calorie-counting approach, or a high-protein regimen, or some new kumquat diet—they all use this same principle to cause weight loss.

The second secret is that there are only three ways of using diet to lose weight. You can limit the number of calories you eat each day by either:

1. Controlling the portions of the food you eat.

2. Adopting a high-protein, low-carbohydrate diet that throws your body into ketosis, a condition associated with starvation that appears to help suppress appetite.

3. Or, eating a low-calorie dense diet.

All of the programs ever invented have utilized one or another of these three ways to create weight loss. Every "new" program that arrives on the market is merely a variation on one of these old themes—all dressed up in new clothes and wrapped in the label "revolutionary."

The third and most dismal little secret is that the first two programs cannot work—that is, they cannot create healthful and sustained weight loss for most people who adopt them. These programs can provide short-term weight loss, which is how they remain in business, but they require tremendous discipline—especially the portion-control programs—and cannot be sustained.

All of which brings us to the fourth secret: Effective, sustained weight loss and good health can only be achieved by adopting what I now call the Calorie Density Solution. In fact, the Calorie Density Solution is an advanced version of the low-fat, high-carbohydrate diet. I say advanced because it identifies the sources of weight gain that still bedevil so many people who adopt high-carbohydrate, low-fat diets but nonetheless have trouble losing weight.

Allow me to summarize very briefly why two of the three approaches fail. I will then show you how you can use the Calorie Density Solution to create good health, including a healthy weight.

PORTION CONTROL: HUNGER, HUNGER, HUNGER

Let's begin with the portion-control or calorie-counting programs. Once you adopt one of these programs, you are free to eat most of the foods on the standard American diet, except those that are exceptionally high in calories. Still, most foods that have a high caloric density are permitted, which means that you very easily can consume high-calorie dense foods, without knowing it. The way portion-control diets get around this problem is by limiting the amount of food you are allowed to eat. That's how they keep your calorie intake down and cause you to lose weight.

Essentially, these diets require you to adopt a kind of modified fast, which means you're hungry all the time. That's why most of us cannot maintain them and why lasting weight loss cannot be achieved. Inevitably, your will power snaps and you start eating. Once that happens, you're likely to keep eating until you restore your sense of satiety, satisfaction, and balance—which, unfortunately, could require a lot of eating, and thus a lot of weight gain.

HIGH-PROTEIN DIETS AND DRINKS: LESS WEIGHT, POORER HEALTH

High-protein diets manipulate your body's metabolism by throwing it into a state of ketosis, an abnormal condition that is associated with starvation. Ketosis is actually a deficiency of carbohydrates in the diet. Once in ketosis, many people experience less hunger. This makes it easier to consume smaller amounts of food, which in turn means that your caloric intake drops. That causes you to start burning fat reserves, which is how you lose weight. Water stored in your tissues is also shed, causing further weight loss.

Interestingly, many high-protein diets eliminate a lot of the most calorically dense foods. The most popular of these regimens prohibit all refined and highly processed foods, such as bread, rolls, fat-free chips, cookies, cakes, dry cereals, crackers, and all foods with refined sugar, such as soft drinks and candy. All of these foods are high in calorie density. In addition, many forms of meat, as I have been showing, are lower in calorie density than many processed carbohydrate foods, which means that, overall, the high protein diet may be lower in calorie density than the foods people were eating when they adopted such a regimen. Combine that lower calorie density diet with a reduction in hunger—caused by the ketosis—and the loss of water and you may indeed experience a certain degree of weight loss, at least initially.

This explains why people who eat out often are the most successful at losing weight on ketogenic diets. They may eat a lobster dipped in butter, a small salad with oil and vinegar, and coleslaw—all of which have a much lower calorie density than bread and butter, French fries, and chocolate cake—foods that are forbidden on high-protein regimens.

Still, there are many significant drawbacks to these programs, the most dangerous of which affect your health. Most high-protein diets are made up of foods that are rich in fat and cholesterol, which of course are associated with heart disease and cancer. High-protein regimens are also low in plant nutrients. Plants are the only source of fiber and the most abundant source of vitamins, minerals, and phytochemicals available to humans. Without them, we can easily become deficient in many essential minerals, vitamins, and phytochemicals. Plants also provide your body with its preferred fuel, carbohydrates, which are restricted on such programs. Because we need a wide variety of plant foods to maintain both health and energy, we end up craving them while we're on high-protein diets.

Without adequate plant foods and carbohydrates in our diets, many people experience a decline in health and acute cravings for carbohydrate-rich foods. This explains why so many people have great difficulty staying on high-protein diets. Ironically, such cravings trigger a carbohydrate binge, which is what often saves people from the most damaging effects of such a diet. Once people eat a carbohydrate-rich food, their bodies are immediately thrown out of ketosis. Hunger for carbohydrate-rich foods returns with a vengeance and people often find themselves gorging on carbohydrate-rich foods—especially processed carbs—which of course cause weight gain.

Even though ketogenic diets usually cause initial weight loss, it's very difficult for most people to maintain such programs. Therefore, sustained weight loss on such programs is virtually impossible for most people. Perhaps it's just as well, since the foods on these diets can lead to serious illness.

THE GLYCEMIC INDEX: ANOTHER FALSE TRAIL

Proponents of some high-protein diets often cite the glycemic index as the principle reason why people should avoid carbohydrate-rich foods and eat mostly high-protein animal foods.

The glycemic index is a tool for measuring how rapidly sugar is absorbed into your bloodstream. Proponents of the glycemic index argue that foods that are rapidly absorbed cause weight retention and weight gain, while those that are slowly absorbed promote weight loss. Unfortunately, it's not as simple as the salespersons make it out to be. Here's why.

When sugars are absorbed more quickly into the bloodstream, the pancreas secretes insulin into the blood. Insulin acts as a kind of gatekeeper, permitting blood sugar to enter cells, where it is used as a fuel. Normally, the fuel mix in your muscle cells is about half fat, half sugar (or glucose).

When higher-than-normal amounts of sugar are absorbed into your bloodstream, the body reacts very quickly to turn down fat-burning and instead burns mostly sugar. While this takes place, however, the muscles are breaking down and burning less fat and more sugar. That, obviously, can be bad for weight loss.

At the same time, fats that are in the blood are stored in the fat cells, as well as the fat that enters the blood via the meal. In other words, high insulin levels cause us to store fat, rather than burn it. Proponents of the glycemic index argue that foods that are rapidly absorbed—and therefore have a high glycemic index score—cause us to burn more sugar and store more fat.

In fact, many carbohydrate-rich foods, especially processed and concentrated carbs, are more rapidly absorbed. These foods are seen as promoting weight gain. High-protein and high-fat foods are more slowly absorbed, in most cases; they are given a lower glycemic index score and are seen as causing weight loss.

Unfortunately, those who tout the glycemic index are fixated exclusively on the rate at which a food's calories are absorbed into the bloodstream. They argue that this single factor, and this one alone, determines a food's effects on your weight. In fact, the rate of absorption can be slowed simply by adding fat. This is the reason why high-fat foods are considered good for weight loss, at least by proponents of the glycemic index. But, obviously, just because a high-fat food is slowly absorbed doesn't mean it will cause you to lose weight—if it's high in calorie density. On the contrary, adding fat to a food will increase its calorie density and raise the likelihood of weight gain.

The glycemic index fails to distinguish between sources of concentrated calories, such as cakes and cookies, and unconcentrated calories, such as carrots and brown rice. When looked at only through the lens of the glycemic index, most carbohydrates are alike, even when they have very different calorie densities. For example, bread and carrots have essentially the same glycemic index score—and both are seen promoting weight gain equally.

However, when looked at through the lens of calorie density, we see that this assertion is ridiculous. Bread has a calorie density of about 1,280 calories per pound. Carrots have a calorie density of 205 calories per pound. Which food do you think is going to cause you to gain more weight?

It gets worse. A Snickers bar, with a calorie density of 2,160 calories per pound, has a lower glycemic index score than oatmeal, which provides 280 calories per pound and has a high satiety value. Yet, the proponents of the glycemic index would have you choose a Snickers bar over oatmeal to "lower" your weight.

To their credit, the proponents of the glycemic index have encouraged people to avoid processed and concentrated carbohydrate foods, such as dried cereals, bagels, and rolls. But telling people to avoid carrots and oatmeal because they cause weight gain is about as intelligent as telling people to eat sausage for their health. And by the way, sausage has a lower glycemic index than a baked potato.

The glycemic index is like an unguided missile: sometimes it hits the target, but a lot of the time it hits an innocent bystander. Because this is such an imprecise tool—and I use the term "tool" loosely—it doesn't guide us accurately on which foods will cause weight gain and which ones won't.

The only way that the glycemic index has any value is when it is used to compare foods of similar calorie densities, such as a baked potato and a sweet potato. Both have a calorie density of about 490 calories per pound. In that case, the food that is more slowly absorbed—the sweet potato— may be preferred as the one that will be slightly better for your weight. However, when dealing with foods with vastly different calorie densities, such as carrots and cheese, the glycemic index has no relevance and cannot guide you to making a healthy choice.

HIGH-CARBOHYDRATE, LOW-FAT DIETS: THE SOLUTION—IF YOU DO THEM RIGHT

Ideally, diets rich in carbohydrates and low in fat rely primarily on whole, natural plant foods, such as vegetables, fruit, beans, and grains. Some programs, such as our own, include low-fat animal products, as well. Ideally, this diet should be composed of low-calorie dense foods that provide feelings of fullness and satisfaction, thanks to the water and fiber.

Unfortunately, as we have already seen, the words "high carbohydrate, low fat" do not necessarily mean low in calorie density, as it once did. Too many people today think that they can lose weight by eating dried and processed high-carbohydrate foods, which is almost impossible. Technically, these are high-carbohydrate foods, but they are way too high in calorie density to cause anything but weight gain. Thus, even as people keep the fat content of their diets low, they are still gaining weight.

THE SOLUTION THAT WORKS

Chronic hunger, food cravings, poor health, and confusion are the undoing of diets today. So much of what we know about dieting—especially what we've learned from experience—makes us realize that the odds are stacked against us when we try to lose weight. But there is a way to consume fewer calories than you burn each day and at the same time avoid all the pitfalls—such as hunger and poor health—that normally derail other diets. That way is the Calorie Density Solution. As we practice this approach, we must also keep in mind that dieting affects not just your weight, but your health, which means it affects every aspect of your life.

The Pritikin Program is the most effective diet-and-exercise approach ever created for overcoming heart disease, high blood pressure, adult-onset diabetes, other serious disorders, and overweight. Our program is the most thoroughly studied and documented diet- and-health regimen available today. University scientists have evaluated our results and published more than 70 scientific studies in peer-reviewed medical journals.

If you follow the recommendations outlined in this book, you can regain your optimal weight, experience abundant energy, and restore normal function to vital organs, such as your heart and digestive tract. Many people with serious degenerative illnesses, such as heart disease, adult-onset diabetes, and high blood pressure, will find the symptoms of these illnesses disappearing. Those with circulatory disorders and joint pain will very likely experience a reduction or elimination of that pain. You'll likely sleep deeper and wake up more refreshed. By following this program, you can witness an antiaging process that causes you to look and feel years younger than you look and feel right now. In short, it can transform every aspect of your life.

The program can accomplish these goals without causing feelings of deprivation or hunger. Once you become accustomed to the foods on the Pritikin Program and start to experience their effects on your health, the quality of your life will improve dramatically.

CASE IN POINT: SHUNSAKU SUGIURA'S STORY

At the age of 50, Shunsaku (Shuny) Sugiura was 60 pounds overweight. That may have been the least of his problems, however. His blood cholesterol level, for which he was taking medication, was dangerously high. He had hypertension, for which he was also taking medication, and adult-onset diabetes. His blood sugar was so high, in fact, that even when he was taking the maximum oral medication, it still hovered between 300 and 400 mg/dl, well into the diabetic range (126 mg/dl or higher; normal blood sugar is below 110 mg/dl). His doctors told him that he must begin taking insulin, but Shuny refused. A self-employed software programmer with his own consulting firm, Shuny had already seen many people in his profession in similar circumstances and had observed the effects of insulin on his colleagues, the most obvious of which was to create significant weight gain. "I didn't want to take insulin," he said recently. "From what I'd seen in my field—from other diabetics like me who traveled all the time and worked 60 to 80 hours a week—insulin was a career breaker."

Shuny hunted for alternatives via the internet. He wanted to find a single program that addressed his many illnesses. "I discovered a whole bunch of candidates," he said, "but Pritikin was the only one I could find that had integrated everything."

Just over a year ago, Shuny came to the Pritikin Longevity Center and experienced a transformation even he didn't expect. Five months after starting the program, he was off all cholesterol medication. Five months after that, he was off all medication for diabetes. As his doctor told him, Shuny is "essentially a nondiabetic." He's also 60 pounds lighter. "I'm the same weight that I was at 28," he told us recently. He's also in the best shape he's been in since he was young. Five days a week, he works out on his treadmill and whenever he travels he walks on the treadmills at hotels and local health clubs.

All of these changes have brought more than physical health, Shuny tells us. "This past year, I've gone from being a pessimist to an optimist. All things are possible. The healthier I've become, the more hopeful and rewarding my life is."

MARGARET'S STORY

At 36 years of age, Margaret Olson weighed 223 pounds and essentially thought the rest of her life would be one long misery. "Every one of my joints ached. I moved like an old woman," she recalled. The first week she was on the Pritikin Program, she didn't think she could do two weeks. "There's just no way I'm going to be able to do this," she told her husband, George. By the second week, her attitude made a 180 degree turn. "There's no way I'm not going to do this," she said.

The reason for her drastic turnabout was simple: results. Her energy levels jumped dramatically. She lost four pounds but realized that she felt a great deal lighter than her weight loss might indicate. A month later, the pain in her joints had diminished dramatically and she was consistently shedding pounds. Now two years on the program, Margaret has lost 75 pounds and is healthier and happier than she's ever been. "I never thought I could feel and look this good. I was heavy my whole life and if it wasn't for the pain in my joints, I would have lived out the rest of my life overweight. But I had to do something. Now the pain is gone and so is my weight. I'm going to do this for the rest of my life. It's the only way to live."

5 | THE PRITIKIN PROGRAM'S CALORIE DENSITY SOLUTION

In this chapter, we provide an extensive array of meal choices for home and when eating in restaurants. The home menu guide provides seven days' worth of menus for breakfast, lunch, and dinner, with three menu choices for each meal. There are seven days' worth of snacks, as well.

Each meal falls under one of three categories, Better, Better Still, and Best, which reflect the meal's quality according to its calorie density. A Better choice has a lower calorie density than the standard American choice for that meal. Better Still provides an even lower calorie density, and Best provides an ideal calorie density choice for weight loss. In addition to providing the calorie density for each meal, we also give you the meal's total ounces and total calories.

As you progress from the Better meals to those under Better Still and to the Best choices, you'll find that with each step upward in quality, the total weights of the meal go up, while the total calories and the calorie densities go down. This means that as you move from Better to Better Still to Best, your meals become more filling, as the total calories and the calorie densities of your meals go down. This combination, of course, will increase satiety and promote weight loss. You'll find this same pattern occurring throughout the menus for Breakfast, Lunch, Dinner, and Snacks, as well as in the Restaurant Choices.

Let me give you a simple example. Under Snacks, you'll find a Better snack includes a 4-ounce bag of fat-free chips and a diet soda. The snack provides 4 ounces of food—the liquids are not counted because, as I said in Chapter 3, the body handles them differently. The snack contains 305 total calories and has a calorie density of 1,220—hardly a weight loss promoter. A Better Still choice would be 1 medium-size baked potato, 2 tablespoons of fat-free sour cream, and iced tea without sugar. The Better Still snack weighs 8 ounces, provides only 246 calories, and has a calorie density of 484 calories per pound. Not bad, especially since this snack will provide a lot more food and will be a lot more filling than a small bag of chips. But check out the Best selection, which includes 1 small baked potato, 1 tablespoon of fat-free sour cream, 1 cup of raw vegetables, 2 tablespoons of fat-free Italian dressing, and herbal tea. Total ounces: 9. Total calories: 212. Calorie density: 363! That snack, with all that food, not only will fill you up, but it will also promote weight loss.

As long as you exercise and keep the overall calorie density of your meals to 400 calories per pound, or lower, you will be losing weight—as you fill up your stomach at every meal. Each menu provides an array of delicious foods for a particular meal, as well as the total ounces, calories, and calorie density for that meal.

The restaurant meal guide in this chapter provides recommendations for eating out, all based on calorie density. We provide these suggestions for eight types of restaurants: American, Chinese, fast food, French, Italian, Japanese, Mexican, and Thai. Each menu suggestion offers a low-to-moderate calorie density choice. In addition, we make suggestions for ways to lower the calorie density of your meals. As with the home guide menu in this chapter, total ounces, calories, and the calorie density are provided for each meal.

As we pointed out in Chapter 3, liquids are treated differently in the body than are solid foods. Therefore, we have not included liquids in the calorie density figure. Liquids can add calories to your meals without creating fullness or satiety. Therefore, I recommend that you minimize high-calorie drinks, such as soda pop, fruit juices, or alcoholic beverages.

It's a good idea to keep certain key calorie density principles in mind when you prepare meals or order in restaurants. Here are a few reminders of ways to lower the calorie density of your meals.

1. As much as possible, eat whole, unprocessed grains, vegetables, beans, and fruits, all of which are lower in calorie density. Limit your intake of foods whose calories have been dried and concentrated during processing.

2. Foods that contain water and fiber tend to be lower in calorie density than those that have been dried. For example, oatmeal, pasta, and tofu, although processed, tend to be lower in calorie density than most dried foods, such as bread, rolls, and crackers. Therefore, the former foods are better choices for both weight loss than the latter.

3. Eat foods low in fat. Fat is the most calorically dense substance in the food supply. Fat-free chips, for example, are preferred over full-fat chips. Choose dressings, sauces, and dips that are fat-free or lower in fat content.

4. To lower a meal's overall calorie density, add low-calorie dense foods to the meal. The best way to do that is by adding vegetables, vegetable dips, such as salsa, or bean dip with salsa. Remember the example I gave in Chapter 3 in which I added guacamole to chips to lower their calorie density.

5. Whenever you eat a carbohydrate-rich food, such as brown rice or potato, eat at least one vegetable to lower the meal's calorie density. A good way to do that is to add a salad or a vegetable, such as broccoli, carrots, onions, cabbage, spinach, or watercress.

6. Whenever you eat a protein-rich food, especially an animal food, eat two vegetables, such as tomatoes and asparagus.

7. Don't forget to sequence your food selection during your meals. Eat the foods that have the lowest calorie density first. Salads with fat-free dressings, along with vegetable soups, will fill you up while providing very low-calorie dense foods. By eating these low-calorie dense foods first, you are leaving less room in your stomach for the higher-calorie dense foods of your meal.

These rules will lower your meals' calorie densities, as they increase their satiety value. In short, these rules promote fullness and weight loss.

You will see these same principles being applied over and over again in the menu plans and the restaurant guide provided on the following pages. As you use these principles yourself, they will become second nature to you, which will make weight loss and better health as simple as eating.

HOME MENU GUIDE

Breakfast

DAY	BETTER	BETTER STILL	BEST
1	• 3 pancakes cooked in reduced-fat butter spray • 3 Tbsp. syrup • 3 tsp. margarine • 1 banana • 8 ounces 1% milk • 1 cup decaf coffee	• 1 English Muffin • 2 Tbsp. low-fat cream cheese • 1 cup strawberries • 1 cup low-fat fruit yogurt • 1 cup decaf tea	• 1⅓ cups oatmeal with cinnamon • 1 cup blueberries • 1 banana • 8 ounces nonfat milk • 1 cup herbal tea
	Total ounces: 10 Total calories: 537 **Caloric density: 904**	Total ounces: 16 Total calories: 482 **Caloric density: 481**	Total ounces: 20 Total calories: 376 **Caloric density: 299**
2	• Egg Substitute Omelet (equivalent of 2 eggs) cooked in reduced-fat butter spray • 2 slices Canadian bacon • 2 slices raisin toast • 2 tsp. margarine • 2 tsp. jam • 4 ounces low-sodium V8 juice • 1 cup decaf coffee	• Egg Substitute Omelet (equivalent of 2 eggs) cooked in Pam • 1 slice whole-wheat toast • 1 Tbsp. fat-free cheddar cheese • 1 fresh orange • 1 cup decaf tea	• Egg Substitute Omelet (equivalent of 2 eggs) cooked in Pam with: -1 cup diced red potatoes -½ cup diced onion • 1 cup strawberries • 1 cup herbal tea
	Total ounces: 8 Total calories: 351 **Caloric density: 688**	Total ounces: 11 Total calories: 294 **Caloric density: 413**	Total ounces: 18 Total calories: 267 **Caloric density: 241**

Total ounces, total calories, and caloric density (CD) do not include liquids.

Breakfast

DAY	BETTER	BETTER STILL	BEST
3	• 1 low-fat blueberry muffin • 2 tsp. margarine • 1 banana • 8 ounces low-fat fruit yogurt • 8 ounces 1% milk • 1 cup decaf coffee	• 1 bagel • 2 Tbsp. fat-free cream cheese • 1 slice tomato • 1 banana • 1 cup fat-free yogurt • 1 cup decaf tea	• 1⅓ cups hot 7-grain cereal • 1 cup sliced peaches • 8 ounces nonfat milk • 1 cup fresh fruit (mixed) • 1 cup herbal tea
	Total ounces: 11 Total calories: 505 **Caloric density: 732**	Total ounces: 17 Total calories: 454 **Caloric density: 433**	Total ounces: 32 Total calories: 415 **Caloric density: 207**
4	• 3 frozen low-fat waffles • 3 Tbsp. light maple syrup • 3 tsp. margarine • 1 sliced banana • 1 cup decaf coffee	• 1 cup Cream of Wheat • 8 ounces 1% milk • 1 slice whole-wheat toast • 1 Tbsp. jam • 1 banana • 1 cup decaf tea	• 1⅓ cups hot Irish oatmeal • 1 sliced banana • 1 cup fresh fruit salad • 8 ounces nonfat milk • 1 cup herbal tea
	Total ounces: 10 Total calories: 484 **Caloric density: 799**	Total ounces: 15 Total calories: 411 **Caloric density: 428**	Total ounces: 24 Total calories: 370 **Caloric density: 251**

Breakfast

DAY	BETTER	BETTER STILL	BEST
5	• Egg Substitute Omelet (equivalent of 2 eggs) cooked in reduced-fat butter spray • 2 ounces fat-free cheese • 2 slices whole-wheat toast • 2 Tbsp. jam • 2 tsp. margarine • 1 cup decaf coffee	• 1 cup instant oatmeal with cinnamon • 1 sliced banana • 8 ounces 1% milk • 1/8 melon • 1 cup decaf tea	• 1 cup Wheatena • 6 ounces nonfat yogurt • 1 cup strawberries • 1 banana • 1 cup herbal tea
	Total ounces: 11 Total calories: 369 **Caloric density: 521**	Total ounces: 18 Total calories: 304 **Caloric density: 273**	Total ounces: 24 Total calories: 287 **Caloric density: 193**
6	• 3 blueberry pancakes cooked in reduced-fat butter spray • 3 Tbsp. light maple syrup • 3 tsp. margarine • 8 ounces 1% milk • 1 cup decaf coffee	• 3 buckwheat pancakes • Nonfat butter spray • 1 sliced banana • 1 cup fresh strawberries • 1 cup decaf tea	• 3 oat bran apple pancakes • 3 Tbsp. sugar-free syrup • 1 sliced banana • 1 grapefruit • 1 cup herbal tea
	Total ounces: 10 Total calories: 627 **Caloric density: 1,035**	Total ounces: 17 Total calories: 602 **Caloric density: 575**	Total ounces: 23 Total calories: 500 **Caloric density: 356**

Total ounces, total calories, and caloric density (CD) do not include liquids.

Breakfast

DAY	BETTER	BETTER STILL	BEST
7	• 2 ounces Corn Flakes • 8 ounces 1% milk • 2 slices whole-wheat toast • 2 Tbsp. jam • 2 tsp. margarine • 1 cup decaf coffee	• 2 ounces Raisin Bran • 8 ounces 1% milk • 1 sliced banana • ½ cup nonfat cottage cheese • 1 cup decaf tea	• 3 biscuits Shredded Wheat • 8 ounces nonfat milk • 1 cup strawberries • 1 cup blueberries • 1 cup herbal tea
	Total ounces: 6 Total calories: 365 **Caloric density: 975**	Total ounces: 10 Total calories: 347 **Caloric density: 562**	Total ounces: 12 Total calories: 339 **Caloric density: 445**

Lunch

DAY	BETTER	BETTER STILL	BEST
1	• 3½ ounces roast beef • French roll • 2 Tbsp. mustard • 2 ounces fat-free chips • Iced tea or diet soda	• 3½ ounces grilled chicken breast • Hard roll • 2 cups salad • 2 Tbsp. reduced-fat dressing • Diet soda	• 3½ ounces grilled chicken breast • 1 ear of corn • 2 cups salad • 2 Tbsp. fat-free dressing • Mineral water or herbal tea
	Total ounces: 8 Total calories: 580 **Caloric density: 1,181**	Total ounces: 15 Total calories: 490 **Caloric density: 539**	Total ounces: 18 Total calories: 428 **Caloric density: 375**
2	• Chicken burrito: -3½ ounces chicken breast -½ cup white rice -¼ cup salsa -3 slices avocado -1 flour tortilla • Iced tea or diet soda	• Bean and rice burrito: -½ cup fat-free refried beans -½ cup white rice -¼ cup salsa -1 corn tortilla • 2 slices cantaloupe • Chinese tea or mineral water	• Vegetable burrito: -1 cup steamed vegetables -½ cup brown rice -¼ cup salsa -1 corn tortilla • 2 cups salad • 2 Tbsp. balsamic vinegar • Mineral water or herbal tea
	Total ounces: 10 Total calories: 450 **Caloric density: 758**	Total ounces: 12 Total calories: 395 **Caloric density: 513**	Total ounces: 19 Total calories: 307 **Caloric density: 252**

Total ounces, total calories, and caloric density (CD) do not include liquids.

Lunch

DAY	BETTER	BETTER STILL	BEST
3	• 5 ounces ham, 95% fat-free, extra lean • 2 slices nonfat cheese • 1 ounce reduced-fat chips • 1 roll • 3 fat-free cookies • 8 ounces 1% milk	• 5 ounces fresh turkey breast • 2 slices nonfat cheese • 2 Tbsp. mustard • 1 roll • 1 cup nonfat cottage cheese • 1/2 cup sliced peaches • Diet soda	• 3 1/2 ounces tuna (canned in water) • 1/4 cup fat-free mayonnaise • 1 whole-wheat pita bread • 2 cups raw vegetables • 1/4 cup nonfat Italian dressing • 1 cup watermelon • Mineral water
	Total ounces: 11 Total calories: 638 **Caloric density: 963**	Total ounces: 23 Total calories: 608 **Caloric density: 427**	Total ounces: 27 Total calories: 503 **Caloric density: 294**
4	• Peanut butter and jelly sandwich -2 Tbsp. peanut butter -2 Tbsp. jam -2 slices whole-wheat bread • 1/2 cup unsweetened applesauce • 8 ounces 1% milk	• 1 Veggie or Garden Burger • 1 whole-wheat bun • 1 slice nonfat cheese • 2 cups salad • 2 Tbsp. reduced-fat dressing • 2 fat-free cookies • Diet soda	• 1 cup fat-free vegetarian chili • 1/2 cup brown rice • 2 cups steamed vegetables • 1 orange • Decaf iced tea or sugar-free lemonade
	Total ounces: 10 Total calories: 595 **Caloric density: 943**	Total ounces: 14 Total calories: 483 **Caloric density: 540**	Total ounces: 27 Total calories: 431 **Caloric density: 250**

Lunch

DAY	BETTER	BETTER STILL	BEST
5	• 2 soft tortillas • 3½ ounces chicken breast • ¼ cup shredded lettuce • ¼ cup chopped tomato • ½ cup fat-free refried beans • ½ cup white rice • Iced tea or diet soda Total ounces: 14 Total calories: 577 **Caloric density: 639**	• 1 slice cheeseless vegetable pizza (a 10-ounce slice) • 2 cups salad • 2 Tbsp. reduced-fat salad dressing • Diet soda Total ounces: 19 Total calories: 529 **Caloric density: 445**	• 3½ ounces broiled fish • 1 baked potato • 2 Tbsp. nonfat sour cream • 2 cups salad • 2 Tbsp. fat-free dressing • ½ cup fresh fruit salad • Mineral water Total ounces: 25 Total calories: 500 **Caloric density: 316**
6	• Stir-fry: -5 ounces beef -½ cup broccoli -1 cup steamed rice • 2 almond cookies • Chinese tea Total ounces: 11 Total calories: 491 **Caloric density: 743**	• Stir-fry: -5 ounces chicken breast -2 cups stir-fried vegetables -½ cup steamed rice • 1 fortune cookie • Chinese tea Total ounces: 19 Total calories: 438 **Caloric density: 351**	• Stir-fry: -5 ounces firm tofu -2 cups steamed vegetables -½ cup brown rice • ½ cup pineapple slices in water • Herbal tea or mineral water Total ounces: 27 Total calories: 386 **Caloric density: 231**

Total ounces, total calories, and caloric density (CD) do not include liquids.

Lunch

DAY	BETTER	BETTER STILL	BEST
7	• 3½ ounces processed turkey • 1 hard roll • 2 Tbsp. mustard • 1 ounce low-fat cheese • 2 leaves lettuce • 2 tomato slices • 2 ounces twisted, thin, pretzels • Iced tea	• 3½ ounces fresh turkey breast • 1 sourdough roll • 2 Tbsp. mustard • 2 leaves lettuce • 2 slices tomato • 1 cup salad • 1 Tbsp. reduced-fat dressing • 1 ounce sourdough pretzels • Diet soda	• 3½ ounces fresh turkey breast • 2 slices whole-wheat bread • 2 Tbsp. mustard • 2 leaves lettuce • 2 slices tomato • 1 cup salad • 1 Tbsp. fat-free Italian dressing • ½ cup berries • Mineral water
	Total ounces: 11 Total calories: 616 **Caloric density: 874**	Total ounces: 14 Total calories: 498 **Caloric density: 557**	Total ounces: 17 Total calories: 460 **Caloric density: 431**

Dinner

DAY	BETTER	BETTER STILL	BEST
1	• 1½ cups chili con carne with beans • 6 reduced-fat crackers • 1 cup salad • 1 Tbsp. reduced-fat dressing • 12 ounces light beer	• 1½ cups low-fat chili • 1 cup brown rice • 1 cup lettuce and tomato salad • 1 Tbsp. reduced-fat dressing • Iced tea or diet soda	• 1½ cups fat-free vegetarian chili • ½ cup brown rice • 2 cups tomato and cucumber salad • 2 Tbsp. balsamic vinegar • ½ cup pineapple slices (in water) • Mineral water
	Total ounces: 19 Total calories: 634 **Caloric density: 544**	Total ounces: 25 Total calories: 473 **Caloric density: 298**	Total ounces: 32 Total calories: 439 **Caloric density: 220**
2	• 1½ cups white pasta • 1 cup marinara sauce • 1 Tbsp. Parmesan cheese • 1 cup salad • 1 Tbsp. reduced-fat dressing • 1 slice sourdough bread • 1 slice Entenmann's fat-free carrot cake (⅛ cake) • 1 glass dry wine	• Chicken teriyaki rice bowl with: -2 ounces chicken breast -1½ cups white rice -2 Tbsp. teriyaki sauce • 1 cup salad • 1 Tbsp. reduced-fat dressing • 8 ounces low-fat yogurt • 1 cup strawberries • Iced tea or diet soda	• 3½ ounces poached salmon • 5 or 6 roasted new potatoes • ½ cup asparagus • 2 cups salad • 2 Tbsp. balsamic vinegar • ½ cup fruit salad • Hot herbal tea
	Total ounces: 24 Total calories: 828 **Caloric density: 557**	Total ounces: 26 Total calories: 677 **Caloric density: 423**	Total ounces: 28 Total calories: 496 **Caloric density: 283**

* Recipe is included in Chapter 10.
Total ounces, total calories, and caloric density (CD) do not include liquids.

Dinner

DAY	BETTER	BETTER STILL	BEST
3	• 1½ cups Chicken Vegetable Curry*	• ½ cup Chicken Vegetable Curry*	• 1½ cups Italian Vegetable Stew*
	• 1 cup white rice	• ½ cup brown rice	• 2 cups salad
	• 1 cup salad	• 1 cup salad	• 2 Tbsp. fat-free dressing
	• 1 Tbsp. reduced-fat dressing	• 1 Tbsp. reduced-fat dressing	• 1 cup fresh fruit salad
	• 2 fat-free cookies	• ½ cup fat-free chocolate pudding	• 1 cup fat-free plain yogurt
	• ½ cup nonfat frozen yogurt	• Hot herbal tea	• Hot herbal tea
	• Hot herbal tea		
	Total ounces: 21 Total calories: 587 **Caloric density: 447**	Total ounces: 22 Total calories: 521 **Caloric density: 372**	Total ounces: 39 Total calories: 494 **Caloric density: 202**

Dinner

DAY	BETTER	BETTER STILL	BEST
4	• 1½ cups white linguine with quick clam sauce: -½ cup marinara sauce -3½ ounces minced clams -1 Tbsp. olive oil • 1 cup salad • 1 Tbsp. reduced-fat dressing • 1 slice sourdough bread • 1 fat-free brownie • 1 glass dry wine	• 1½ cups white linguine with quick clam sauce (no oil) • 1 cup salad • 1 Tbsp. reduced-fat dressing • ½ cup applesauce, sweetened • Diet soda	• 1½ cups whole-wheat pasta • ½ cup marinara sauce • 3½ ounces clams • 2 cups salad • 2 Tbsp. fat-free dressing • 1 cup strawberries • Mineral water
	Total ounces: 22 Total calories: 781 **Caloric density: 567**	Total ounces: 25 Total calories: 586 **Caloric density: 382**	Total ounces: 29 Total calories: 573 **Caloric density: 308**

* Recipe is included in Chapter 10.

Total ounces, total calories, and caloric density (CD) do not include liquids.

Dinner

DAY	BETTER	BETTER STILL	BEST
5	• 1½ cups beef and vegetable stew (prepared with lean top sirloin) • 1 hard roll • 1 cup salad • 1 Tbsp. reduced-fat dressing • 1 slice fat-free iced chocolate cake (Entenmann's) • 1 cup decaf coffee	• 1½ cups Jamaican Fish Stew* • 1 ear of corn • 1 cup salad • 1 Tbsp. reduced-fat dressing • ½ cup nonfat frozen yogurt • Diet soda	• 1½ cups Winter Squash Stew* • 2 cups salad • 2 Tbsp. fat-free dressing • 1 fresh peach • Hot herbal tea
	Total ounces: 22 Total calories: 785 **Caloric density: 558**	Total ounces: 23 Total calories: 513 **Caloric density: 361**	Total ounces: 27 Total calories: 376 **Caloric density: 225**
6	• 1½ cups cous cous • 3½ ounces grilled chicken breast • ½ cup grilled vegetables • 1 pita, 6½-inch diameter • 2 fat-free cookies • 1 cup decaf coffee	• 1½ cups cous cous • 2 cups grilled vegetables • 1 whole-wheat pita • 1 cup salad • 1 Tbsp. reduced-fat dressing • Diet soda	• 1 serving Orange Rice Pilaf* • 1 cup steamed broccoli • 2 cups salad • 2 Tbsp. fat-free dressing • ½ cup fat-free tapioca pudding • 1 banana sliced • Hot herbal tea
	Total ounces: 18 Total calories: 703 **Caloric density: 622**	Total ounces: 27 Total calories: 625 **Caloric density: 369**	Total ounces: 30 Total calories: 507 **Caloric density: 274**

Dinner

DAY	BETTER	BETTER STILL	BEST
7	• Stir-fry: -3½ ounces pork tenderloin -1 cup steamed vegetables -2 tsp. oil • 1 cup white rice • ½ cup orange sherbet • Hot herbal tea	• Stir-fry: -3½ ounces chicken breast -1 cup steamed vegetables -1 tsp. oil • 1 cup white rice • ½ cup fat-free, sugar-free pudding • Hot herbal tea	• 3½ ounces grilled chicken breast • 1 cup steamed asparagus tips • 1 cup brown rice • 1½ cups salad • 2 Tbsp. vinegar • 1 cup berries • Hot herbal tea
	Total ounces: 17 Total calories: 684 **Caloric density: 647**	Total ounces: 22 Total calories: 653 **Caloric density: 482**	Total ounces: 26 Total calories: 340 **Caloric density: 211**

Total ounces, total calories, and caloric density (CD) do not include liquids.

Snacks

DAY	BETTER	BETTER STILL	BEST
1	• 3 ounces baked tortilla chips • Iced tea	• 2 ounces baked tortilla chips • 2 ounces guacamole • Diet soda	• 2 ounces baked tortilla chips • 1 cup salsa • Herbal tea
	Total ounces: 3 Total calories: 360 **Caloric density: 1,920**	Total ounces: 4 Total calories: 300 **Caloric density: 1,200**	Total ounces: 7 Total calories: 276 **Caloric density: 679**
2	• 3 ounces fat-free crackers • Diet soda	• 2 ounces fat-free crackers • 2 ounces fat-free cheese • Herbal tea	• 2 ounces fat-free crackers • 1 ounce fat-free cheese • 3 tomato slices • Mineral water
	Total ounces: 3 Total calories: 300 **Caloric density: 1,600**	Total ounces: 4 Total calories: 275 **Caloric density: 1,100**	Total ounces: 5 Total calories: 213 **Caloric density: 665**
3	• 1 whole-wheat bagel • 2 Tbsp. light cream cheese • 8 ounces 1% milk	• 1 whole-wheat bagel • 2 Tbsp. fat-free cream cheese • Diet soda	• ½ whole-wheat bagel • 1 Tbsp. fat-free Italian dressing • 1 orange • Herbal tea
	Total ounces: 4 Total calories: 266 **Caloric density: 1,197**	Total ounces: 4 Total calories: 225 **Caloric density: 1,014**	Total ounces: 6 Total calories: 172 **Caloric density: 434**

Snacks

DAY	BETTER	BETTER STILL	BEST
4	• 4 ounces fat-free potato chips • Diet soda	• 1 medium baked potato • 2 Tbsp. fat-free sour cream • Iced tea	• 1 small baked potato • 1 Tbsp. fat-free sour cream • 1 cup raw vegetables • 2 Tbsp. fat-free sour cream • Herbal tea
	Total ounces: 4 Total calories: 305 **Caloric density: 1,220**	Total ounces: 8 Total calories: 246 **Caloric density: 484**	Total ounces: 9 Total calories: 212 **Caloric density: 363**
5	• 8 ounces low-fat fruit yogurt • ¼ cup Grape Nuts • Mineral water	• 8 ounces fat-free, sugar-free yogurt • 1 sliced banana • Iced tea	• 8 ounces fat-free, sugar-free yogurt • ½ sliced banana • ½ cup sliced strawberries • Herbal tea
	Total ounces: 9 Total calories: 336 **Caloric density: 597**	Total ounces: 12 Total calories: 209 **Caloric density: 275**	Total ounces: 13 Total calories: 174 **Caloric density: 223**
6	• 3 ounces fat-free crackers • 8 ounces 1% milk	• 2 ounces fat-free crackers • 3 ounces Broccomole* • Diet soda	• 1 ounce fat-free crackers • 3 ounces Broccomole* • 5 cherry tomatoes
	Total ounces: 3 Total calories: 300 **Caloric density: 1,600**	Total ounces: 5 Total calories: 243 **Caloric density: 778**	Total ounces: 7 Total calories: 161 **Caloric density: 368**

* Recipe is included in Chapter 10.
Total ounces, total calories, and caloric density (CD) do not include liquids.

Snacks

DAY	BETTER	BETTER STILL	BEST
7	• 2 soft pretzels • 1 Tbsp. mustard • Diet soda	• 1 soft pretzel • 1 Tbsp. mustard • 1 pear • Herbal tea	• 1 soft pretzel • 1 Tbsp. mustard • 1½ cups salad • 1 Tbsp. fat-free Italian dressing • Mineral water
	Total ounces: 6 Total calories: 392 **Caloric density: 1,141**	Total ounces: 9 Total calories: 302 **Caloric density: 546**	Total ounces: 10 Total calories: 280 **Caloric density: 439**

RESTAURANT MENU GUIDE

American Dish 1

AS ORDERED	CD	SLIGHT SUBSTITUTION	CD	MAJOR SUBSTITUTION	CD
• 2 cups Green Salad	150	• 2 cups Green Salad	150	• 2 cups Green Salad	150
• 2 Tbsp. blue cheese dressing	2,286	• 2 Tbsp. low-fat dressing	1,310	• 4 Tbsp. Non Fat dressing	650
• 2 pieces Fried Chicken	1,006	• 2 pieces Roasted Chicken	893	• 3 ounces Grilled Chicken	846
• 1/2 cup Corn	489	• 1 cup Corn	489	• 1 cup Corn	489
• 1 cup Mashed Potatoes 2 Tbsp. butter	480 3,252	• 1 cup Carrots	207	• 1 cup Carrots	204
• 1 slice Apple Pie	1,202	• 1 Baked Potato 2 Tbsp. sour cream	494 971	• 1 cup Boiled Potatoes	394
• 1 cup Ice Cream	1,093	• 1 slice Apple Pie	1,202	• 1 cup Apple slices	267

Total ounces: 37
Total calories of meal: 1,936
Caloric density of meal: 819

Total ounces: 41
Total calories of meal: 1,493
Caloric density of meal: 580

Total ounces: 42
Total calories of meal: 1,135
Caloric density of meal: 430

Total ounces, total calories, and caloric density (CD) do not include liquids.

American Dish 2

AS ORDERED	CD	SLIGHT SUBSTITUTION	CD	MAJOR SUBSTITUTION	CD
• 3 slices bread	1,242	• 3 slices bread	1,242	• 1 cup salad -2 Tbsp. fat-free dressing	150 650
• 3 Tbsp. butter	3,252	• 1 Tbsp. butter	3,252		
• 1 cup Cream of Broccoli Soup	378	• 1 cup Minestrone Soup	154	• 1 cup Vegetable Soup	194
• 12 ounces Steak	1,401	• 8 ounces Steak	1,401	• 4 ounces Steak	1,401
• 1 cup Mashed Potatoes	480	• 1 Baked Potato	494	• 1 Baked Potato	494
		• 1 Tbsp. butter	3,252	• 1/2 cup marinara sauce	258
		• 1 cup Carrots	204	• 1 cup Asparagus	108
• 1 slice Chocolate Layer Cake	1,492	• 1 slice Sponge Cake	1,347	• 1 slice Angel Food Cake	1,165
				• 1 cup Strawberries	136

Total ounces: 33
Total calories of meal: 2,208
Caloric density of meal: 1,045

Total ounces: 34
Total calories of meal: 1,657
Caloric density of meal: 770

Total ounces: 42
Total calories of meal: 1,028
Caloric density of meal: 396

American Dish 3

AS ORDERED	CD	SLIGHT SUBSTITUTION	CD	MAJOR SUBSTITUTION	CD

• 3 Egg Omelet
  1 Tbsp. butter
	752
	3,252
		• 3 Egg Omelet
		  (cooked in Pam)
		  -½ cup vegetables
			752
			
			267
				• ¾ cup Egg Beaters
				  (cooked in Pam)
				  -1½ cups Vegetables
					223
					
					267

• 2 slices Bacon	2,612	• 2 pieces Canadian Bacon	839	• 1 cup Oatmeal	281

• 2 cups Hash Browns	1,029	• 2 pieces Toast
		  -2 Tbsp. butter
		  -2 Tbsp. jam
			1,383
			3,252
			1,097
				• 1 Banana	417

• 2 pieces Toast
  -2 Tbsp. butter
  -2 Tbsp. jam
	1,383
	3,252
	1,097
				• 1 Orange	213

Total ounces: 19	Total ounces: 22	Total ounces: 35
Total calories of meal: 1,487	Total calories of meal: 1,094	Total calories of meal: 592
Caloric density of meal: 1,195	**Caloric density of meal: 764**	**Caloric density of meal: 269**

Chinese Dish 1

AS ORDERED	CD	SLIGHT SUBSTITUTION	CD	MAJOR SUBSTITUTION	CD
• 2 Meat Egg Rolls	804	• 2 Vegetable Egg Rolls	717	• 2 Vegetable Egg Rolls	717

• 1 cup Sweet
  and Sour Pork
	750	• 1 cup Moo
		  Goo Gai Pan
			275	• 1 cup Moo
				  Goo Gai Pan
					275

• 2 cups Fried Rice
  with Pork
	754	• 2 cups Vegetable
		  Fried Rice
			416	• 1 cup Mixed
				  Vegetables
					267

• 2 Fortune Cookies	1,714	• 2 Fortune Cookies	1,714	• 1 cup Steamed Rice	517
		• ½ cup Lychee Nuts	299	• 1 cup Orange Slices	213

Total ounces: 28	Total ounces: 30	Total ounces: 34
Total calories of meal: 1,401	Total calories of meal: 825	Total calories of meal: 775
Caloric density of meal: 779	**Caloric density of meal: 437**	**Caloric density of meal: 363**

Total ounces, total calories, and caloric density (CD) do not include liquids.

Chinese Dish 2

AS ORDERED	CD	SLIGHT SUBSTITUTION	CD	MAJOR SUBSTITUTION	CD
• 1 cup Chicken Egg Foo Young	637	• 1 cup Almond Chicken	524	• 1 cup Almond Chicken	524
• 2 cups Fried Rice with Pork	754	• 1 cup Fried Rice with Vegetables	416	• 1 cup Steamed Rice	517
• 1 cup Chow Mein with Chicken	462	• 1 cup Chow Mein with Chicken	462	• 1 cup Mixed Vegetables	267
• 1 Almond Cookie	2,194	• 1 Almond Cookie	2,194	• 1 cup Chow Mein with Chicken	462
				• 1 cup Orange Slices	213

Total ounces: 29
Total calories of meal: 1,194
Caloric density of meal: 654

Total ounces: 32
Total calories of meal: 946
Caloric density of meal: 472

Total ounces: 36
Total calories of meal: 922
Caloric density of meal: 408

Chinese Dish 3

AS ORDERED	CD	SLIGHT SUBSTITUTION	CD	MAJOR SUBSTITUTION	CD
• 2 cups Kung Pao Chicken	1,207	• 1 cup Chow Mein with Chicken	462	• 1 cup Chow Mein with Vegetables	192
• 2 cups Fried Rice	754	• 1 cup Mixed Vegetables	267	• 2 cups Mixed Vegetables	267
• 1 Almond Cookie	2,194	• 1 cup Steamed Rice	517	• 1 cup Steamed Rice	517
		• 1 Fortune Cookie	1,714	• ½ cup Lychee Nuts	299

Total ounces: 25
Total calories of meal: 1,554
Caloric density of meal: 970

Total ounces: 28
Total calories of meal: 697
Caloric density of meal: 397

Total ounces: 31
Total calories of meal: 583
Caloric density of meal: 298

Fast Food *Arby's*

AS ORDERED	CD	SLIGHT SUBSTITUTION	CD	MAJOR SUBSTITUTION	CD
• 1 cup Wisconsin Cheese Soup	559	• 1 cup Boston Clam Chowder	380	• 1 cup Lumberjack Mixed Vegetable Soup	179
• 1 Philly Beef 'n' Swiss Sandwich	1,164	• 1 Roast Beef Sub Sandwich	1,037	• 1 Roasted Chicken Salad	165
• 1 packet Arby's sauce	480	• 1 packet Arby's sauce	480	• 1 packet reduced-fat Italian dressing	646
• 1 Cheddar Curly Fries (3½ ounces fries & ¾ ounce cheddar cheese sauce)	1,258	• 1 Deluxe Baked Potato	773	• Plain Baked Potato	490
		• Diet Soda	N/A	• Bottled water	N/A
• 1 slice Cherry Pie	1,224				
• Regular soda	N/A				

Total ounces: 29
Total calories of meal: 1,856
Caloric density of meal: 1,013

Total ounces: 34
Total calories of meal: 1,629
Caloric density of meal: 760

Total ounces: 39
Total calories of meal: 768
Caloric density of meal: 312

Total ounces, total calories, and caloric density (CD) do not include liquids.

Fast Food *Burger King*

AS ORDERED	CD	SLIGHT SUBSTITUTION	CD	MAJOR SUBSTITUTION	CD
• 1 Chicken Sandwich (fried)	1,406	• 1 BK Broiler Sandwich	973	• 1 BK Broiler Sandwich (no mayo)	680
• 1 medium French Fries	1,564	• 1 small French Fries	1,564	• 1 packet BBQ sauce	648
• 3 packets ketchup	483				
• 1 slice Dutch Apple Pie	1,204	• 1 Garden Salad	211	• 1 small French Fries	1,564
• Regular soda	N/A	• 1 packet light Italian dressing	240	• 1 Garden Salad	211
		• Diet soda	N/A	• 1 packet light Italian dressing	240

Total ounces: 17
Total calories of meal: 1,438
Caloric density of meal: 1,345

Total ounces: 19
Total calories of meal: 885
Caloric density of meal: 717

Total ounces: 20
Total calories of meal: 745
Caloric density of meal: 589

Fast Food *McDonald's (breakfast)*

AS ORDERED	CD	SLIGHT SUBSTITUTION	CD	MAJOR SUBSTITUTION	CD
• 1 Sausage Biscuit with Egg	1,401	• 1 Breakfast Burrito	1,240	• 1 serving Plain Hotcakes	988
• 2 Hash Browns	1,112	• 1 low-fat Apple Bran Muffin	1,193	• 1 serving Maple syrup	1,188
• 1% Low Fat milk	N/A	• 1 Scrambled Egg	711	• 2 Scrambled Eggs	711
		• Orange Juice	N/A	• Tea	N/A

Total ounces: 9
Total calories of meal: 737
Caloric density of meal: 1,314

Total ounces: 10
Total calories of meal: 695
Caloric density of meal: 1,127

Total ounces: 11
Total calories of meal: 604
Caloric density of meal: 920

Fast Food *McDonald's*

AS ORDERED	CD	SLIGHT SUBSTITUTION	CD	MAJOR SUBSTITUTION	CD
• 1 Crispy Chicken Deluxe Sandwich	1,017	• 1 Grilled Chicken Deluxe Sandwich	895	• 1 Grilled Chicken Salad Deluxe	212
• 1 small French Fries	1,391	• 1 small French Fries	1,391	• 1 packet fat-free herb vinaigrette	384
• 2 packets ketchup	483	• 2 packets ketchup	483	• Vanilla (reduced-fat) Ice Cream Cone	756
• 2 bags McDonaldland Cookies	1,944	• 1 slice Baked Apple Pie	1,531	• Bottled water	N/A
• Low-fat milk	N/A	• Diet soda	N/A		

Total ounces: 14
Total calories of meal: 1,086
Caloric density of meal: 1,213

Total ounces: 14
Total calories of meal: 946
Caloric density of meal: 1,063

Total ounces: 16
Total calories of meal: 406
Caloric density of meal: 402

Total ounces, total calories, and caloric density (CD) do not include liquids.

Fast Food *Wendy's*

AS ORDERED	CD	SLIGHT SUBSTITUTION	CD	MAJOR SUBSTITUTION	CD
• 1 Wendy's JR Bacon Cheeseburger	1,038	• 1 Grilled Chicken Sandwich	744	• 1 Deluxe Garden Salad	185
• 1 French Fries, Biggie	1,340	• 1 packet BBQ sauce	729	• 1 packet reduced-fat Italian dressing	646
• 4 packets ketchup	483	• 1 Broccoli and Cheese Baked Potato	518	• 1 Plain Baked Potato	495
• 1 packet Chocolate Chip Cookies	2,148	• Diet soda	N/A	• 1 Large Chili Bowl	413
• Regular soda	N/A			• Iced tea (no sugar)	N/A

Total ounces: 15
Total calories of meal: 1,157
Caloric density of meal: 1,256

Total ounces: 22
Total calories of meal: 824
Caloric density of meal: 595

Total ounces: 33
Total calories of meal: 769
Caloric density of meal: 378

French Dish 1

AS ORDERED	CD	SLIGHT SUBSTITUTION	CD	MAJOR SUBSTITUTION	CD
• 6 spears Asparagus with ¹/₄ cup mayonnaise sauce	69 3,251	• 6 spears Asparagus with 1 Tbsp. low-fat dressing	69 1,310	• 6 spears Asparagus with 1 Tbsp. nonfat dressing 1 tsp. Dijon Mustard	69 650 580
• Fillet of Sole Meuniere: -6 ounces Fillet of Sole -¹/₄ cup butter -¹/₄ cup flour	450 3,252 1,651	• Fillet of Sole Provençal: -6 ounces Fillet of Sole -2 Tbsp. oil -¹/₂ cup tomatoes -2 Tbsp. black olives -2 Tbsp. onion	450 4,009 88 521 173	• Fillet of Sole, grilled dry -2 Tbsp. lemon	450 131
• 1 cup Mixed Vegetables -2 Tbsp. butter	150 3,252	• 1 cup Mixed Vegetables	150	• 2 cups Mixed Vegetables	150
• 1 cup Roasted Potatoes with 1 Tbsp. olive oil	421 4,009	• 1 cup Boiled New Potatoes	219	• 1 cup Boiled New Potatoes	219
• 2 pieces French bread	1,242	• 1 piece French bread	1,242	• 1 piece French bread	1,242
• Crème Brûlée	1,191	• 1 cup Fruit Cobbler	353	• 1 cup Fruit Compote	353
		• 2 Tbsp. whipped cream	1,167		

Total ounces: 33
Total calories of meal: 2,189
Caloric density of meal: 1,054

Total ounces: 41
Total calories of meal: 957
Caloric density of meal: 369

Total ounces: 43
Total calories of meal: 718
Caloric density of meal: 263

Total ounces, total calories, and caloric density (CD) do not include liquids.

French Dish 2

AS ORDERED	CD	SLIGHT SUBSTITUTION	CD	MAJOR SUBSTITUTION	CD
• 1 cup Salad with 1 Tbsp. oil and 1 Tbsp. vinegar	150 4,010 635	• 2 cups Salad with 2 Tbsp. balsamic vinegar and 1 tsp. Dijon mustard	150 635 581	• 2 cups Salad with 2 Tbsp. balsamic vinegar and 1 tsp. Dijon mustard	150 635 581
• Boeuf Bourguignon: -2 cups beef stew -½ cup red wine -¼ pound bacon -4 Tbsp. butter	368 326 2,612 3,252	• 1 Steak au Poivre: -6 ounces steak -2 Tbsp. butter -2 Tbsp. brandy -1 Tbsp. peppercorn	1,401 3,252 1,103 1,156	• 4 ounces Grilled Filet Mignon	1,401
• 1 cup Noodles with 1 Tbsp. butter	603	• 12 Pommes Frites (French Fries)	1,460	• 2 cups Roasted Potatoes	421
• 1 piece French bread -2 Tbsp. butter	1,242 3,252	• 1 piece French bread	1242	• 12 spears Asparagus	69
• ½ cup Vanilla Ice Cream with 2 Wafer Cookies	1,093 2,191	• 12 spears Asparagus	69	• 1 piece French bread	1,242
		• 1 cup Sorbet with 2 Wafer Cookies	467 2,191	• 1 cup Sorbet ½ cup Fresh Berries	467 136

Total ounces: 36 Total calories of meal: 2,288 **Caloric density of meal: 1,000**	Total ounces: 37 Total calories of meal: 1,611 **Caloric density of meal: 699**	Total ounces: 39 Total calories of meal: 986 **Caloric density of meal: 399**

French Dish 3

AS ORDERED	CD	SLIGHT SUBSTITUTION	CD	MAJOR SUBSTITUTION	CD
• 2 cups Green Salad with 2 Tbsp. French dressing	150 1,950	• 2 cups Green Salad with 2 Tbsp. low-fat dressing	150 1,310	• 2 cups Green Salad with 2 Tbsp. nonfat dressing	150 650
• Coquilles St. Jacques: -1 cup scallops -1 cup mushrooms -1/2 cup white wine -1/2 cup cream	482 125 308 591	• 2 cups Bouillabaisse (Mediterranean Fish Stew)	480	• 4 ounces Poached Salmon	512
• 1 cup Buttered Noodles	613	• 1 piece French bread with 2 Tbsp. butter	1,242 3,252	• 1 cup Boiled New Potatoes	219
• 1 piece French bread with 2 Tbsp. butter	1,242 3,252			• 1 cup Mixed Vegetables	150
• 1 piece Tarte aux Poires	572			• 1 piece French bread	1,242
		• 1/2 cup Sliced Pear with Vanilla Sauce	267 1,300	• Sliced Pear with Strawberry Sauce	267 1,152

Total ounces: 36
Total calories of meal: 1,422
Caloric density of meal: 623

Total ounces: 37
Total calories of meal: 1,341
Caloric density of meal: 583

Total ounces: 38
Total calories of meal: 810
Caloric density of meal: 341

Total ounces, total calories, and caloric density (CD) do not include liquids.

Italian Dish 1

AS ORDERED	CD	SLIGHT SUBSTITUTION	CD	MAJOR SUBSTITUTION	CD

• 2 cups Green Salad
  2 Tbsp. olive oil
  2 Tbsp. balsamic
  vinegar
	150
	4,009
	635
		• 2 cups Green Salad
		  2 Tbsp.olive oil
		  2 Tbsp. balsamic
		  vinegar
			150
			4,009
			635
				• 2 cups Green Salad
				  1 Tbsp. balsamic
				  vinegar
					150
					635

• 2 cups Fettuccine
  Alfredo
	926	• Fettuccine Primavera
		  -$\frac{1}{2}$ cup vegetables
		  -1 cup fettuccini
			
			267
			594
				• Fettuccini Primavera
				  -$\frac{1}{2}$ cup Vegetables
				  -1 cup Fettuccini
					
					267
					594

• 1 piece Cheesecake	1,456	• $\frac{1}{2}$ cup Vegetables	267		
		• 1 piece Cheesecake	1,456	• 1$\frac{1}{2}$ cups Vegetables	267
		• 1 cup Strawberries	136	• 1 cup Strawberries	136

Total ounces: 25
Total calories of meal: 1,349
Caloric density of meal: 838

Total ounces: 27
Total calories of meal: 783
Caloric density of meal: 453

Total ounces: 31
Total calories of meal: 539
Caloric density of meal: 275

Italian Dish 2

AS ORDERED	CD	SLIGHT SUBSTITUTION	CD	MAJOR SUBSTITUTION	CD

• 4 slices Roma
  Tomatoes
  $\frac{1}{4}$ cup olive oil
  1 cup mozzerella
	95
	
	4,009
	1,153
		• 2 cups Green Salad
		  1 Tbsp. olive oil
		  1 Tbsp. balsamic
		  vinegar
			150
			4,009
			635
				• 2 cups Green Salad
				  2 Tbsp. balsamic
				  vinegar
					150
					635

• 2 cups Rigatoni with
  1 cup Meat Sauce
	594
	524
		• 1 slice bread	1,242	• 2 cups Rigatoni with
				  $\frac{1}{2}$ cup Marinara
				  Sauce
					594
					112

• 1 slice bread	1,242	• 2 cups Rigatoni with $\frac{1}{2}$ cup Marinara Sauce	594 112	• 1 cup Vegetables	267
• 1 cup Zabaglione	1,186	• 1 cup Zabaglione	1,186	• 1 cup Fresh Berries	136
		• 1 cup Fresh Berries	136		

Total ounces: 29
Total calories of meal: 1,610
Caloric density of meal: 882

Total ounces: 30
Total calories of meal: 837
Caloric density of meal: 442

Total ounces: 34
Total calories of meal: 645
Caloric density of meal: 301

Italian Dish 3

AS ORDERED	CD	SLIGHT SUBSTITUTION	CD	MAJOR SUBSTITUTION	CD
• 3 pieces Alla Salisiccia Pizza	1,290	• 3 pieces Primavera Pizza	1,042	• 3 pieces Primavera Pizza	1,042
• 2 cups Green Salad 2 Tbsp. olive oil 2 Tbsp. balsamic vinegar	150 4,009 635	• 2 cups Green Salad 1 Tbsp. olive oil 1 Tbsp. balsamic vinegar	150 4,009 635	• 2 cups Green Salad 2 Tbsp. balsamic vinegar	150 635
• 1 piece Italian Cheesecake	1,456	• ½ cup Vegetables	267	• 2 cups Vegetables	267
		• 1 cup Sorbet	567		
		• 1 cup Fresh Berries	136	• 1 cup Fresh Berries	136

Total ounces: 25
Total calories of meal: 1,645
Caloric density of meal: 1,022

Total ounces: 31
Total calories of meal: 1,053
Caloric density of meal: 532

Total ounces: 34
Total calories of meal: 880
Caloric density of meal: 406

Total ounces, total calories, and caloric density (CD) do not include liquids.

Japanese Dish

AS ORDERED	CD	SLIGHT SUBSTITUTION	CD	MAJOR SUBSTITUTION	CD
• 1 cup Sunomono	76	• 1 cup Sunomono	76	• 1 cup Sunomono	76
• 3 ounces Shrimp Tempura	749	• 4 pieces Vegetable Tempura	737	• 4 pieces Vegetable Sushi	529
• 4 ounces Baked Chicken	846	• 4 ounces Baked Chicken	846	• 4 ounces Baked Chicken	846
• 1/2 cup Teriyaki Sauce	381	• 1/2 cup Teriyaki Sauce	381	• 1 cup Vegetables	267
• 1 cup Steamed Rice	517	• 1 cup Steamed Rice	517	• 1 cup Steamed Rice	517
• 1/2 cup Orange Slices	213	• 1/2 cup Vegetables	267	• 1 cup Fresh Fruit Medley	175
		• 1 cup Orange Slices	213		

Total ounces: 28
Total calories of meal: 744
Caloric density of meal: 421

Total ounces: 31
Total calories of meal: 728
Caloric density of meal: 371

Total ounces: 32
Total calories of meal: 726
Caloric density of meal: 360

Mexican Dish 1

AS ORDERED	CD	SLIGHT SUBSTITUTION	CD	MAJOR SUBSTITUTION	CD
• 3 cups Tortilla Chips	2,081	• 2 cups Tortilla Chips	2,081	• 2 cups Tortilla Chips 1 cup salsa	2,081 127
• 1 fried Tostada	2,025	• 1 fried Tostada	2,025	• 1 plain Tostada	1,006
-1 cup refried beans	426	-1 cup refried beans	426	-1 cup boiled beans	621
-$^1/_2$ cup cheese	1,826	-$^1/_4$ cup cheese	1,826	-3 cups lettuce	54
-2 cups lettuce	54	-3 cups lettuce	54	-1 cup tomatoes	95
-1 cup shredded beef	958	-1 cup tomatoes	95	-$^1/_2$ cup salsa	127
• 1 serving Fried Ice Cream	1,220	• $^1/_2$ cup Guacamole	2,081	• 1 cup Flan	395
		• $^1/_2$ cup salsa	127	• 1 cup Raspberries	222
		• 1 cup Vanilla Ice Cream	1,093		

Total ounces: 32
Total calories of meal: 2,135
Caloric density of meal: 1,061

Total ounces: 36
Total calories of meal: 1,597
Caloric density of meal: 706

Total ounces: 37
Total calories of meal: 1,213
Caloric density of meal: 516

Total ounces, total calories, and caloric density (CD) do not include liquids.

Mexican Dish 2

AS ORDERED	CD	SLIGHT SUBSTITUTION	CD	MAJOR SUBSTITUTION	CD
• 2 cups Nachos with 1 cup Melted Cheese	2,449 1,826	• 2 cups Nachos with 1 cup Salsa	2,449 127	• 3 Corn Tortillas	1,006
• ¹/₂ cup Guacamole	480	• 1 cup Chili Con Carne	572	• 1 cup Black Beans	598
• 1 cup Chili Con Carne	572	• 2 Tbsp. sour cream	971	• 1 Chicken Burrito	1,280
• 1 Burrito Beef and Cheese	981	• ¹/₄ cup Guacamole	480	• ¹/₂ cup Salsa	127
• 2 Tbsp. sour cream	971	• 1 Beef Burrito	897	• 2 cups Vegetables	267
• 1 Sopaipilla	1,630	• 1 cup Ice Cream	1,093	• 1 cup Sherbet	625
				• 1 cup Pineapple	222

Total ounces: 36
Total calories of meal: 2,979
Caloric density of meal: 1,314

Total ounces: 41
Total calories of meal: 2,912
Caloric density of meal: 1,117

Total ounces: 43
Total calories of meal: 1,488
Caloric density of meal: 551

Mexican Dish 3

AS ORDERED	CD	SLIGHT SUBSTITUTION	CD	MAJOR SUBSTITUTION	CD
• 1 cup Tortilla Chips	2,449	• 1 cup Tortilla Chips	2,449	• 2 Corn Tortillas	1,006
• 1¹/₂ cups Guacamole	480	• 1 cup Salsa	127	• 1 cup Salsa	127
• ¹/₂ cup Refried Beans	426	• 1 Chicken Taco	894	• 1 Chicken Soft Taco	793
• ¹/₂ cup Rice	580	• ¹/₂ cup Boiled Beans	621	• ¹/₂ cup Boiled Beans	621
• 1 Steak Taco	966	• ¹/₂ cup Rice	580	• ¹/₂ cup Rice	580
• 1 slice Key Lime Pie	1,378	• 1 cup Flan	395	• 1 cup Sorbet	467
				• 1 cup Berries	136

Total ounces: 25
Total calories of meal: 1,407
Caloric density of meal: 915

Total ounces: 28
Total calories of meal: 1,219
Caloric density of meal: 694

Total ounces: 35
Total calories of meal: 1,097
Caloric density of meal: 495

Thai Dish 1

AS ORDERED	CD	SLIGHT SUBSTITUTION	CD	MAJOR SUBSTITUTION	CD
• 1 cup Chicken Curry	932	• 1 cup Chicken Curry	932	• 2 cups Green Salad	150
				4 Tbsp. lemon juice	113
• 6 pieces Beef Satay	993	• 1¹/₂ cups Fried Rice	876	• 4 ounces	748
¹/₂ cup peanut sauce	925			Thai Chicken	
				(hold the cashews)	
• 1¹/₂ cups Fried Rice	876	• ¹/₂ cup Mixed Vegetables	267	• 2 cups Mixed Vegetables	267
• 1¹/₂ cups Fried Banana	1,136	• 1 cup Fried Banana	1,136	• 1 cup Brown Rice	503
		• 1 cup Orange Slices	213	• 1 cup Orange Slices	213

Total ounces: 32
Total calories of meal: 1,997
Caloric density of meal: 975

Total ounces: 35
Total calories of meal: 1,714
Caloric density of meal: 781

Total ounces: 40
Total calories of meal: 791
Caloric density of meal: 316

Total ounces, total calories, and caloric density (CD) do not include liquids.

Thai Dish 2

AS ORDERED	CD	SLIGHT SUBSTITUTION	CD	MAJOR SUBSTITUTION	CD
• 2 cups Green Salad	150	• 2 cups Green Salad	150	• 2 cups Green Salad	150
½ cup peanut sauce	925	1 Tbsp. tamarind paste	1,080	4 Tbsp. lemon juice	113
• 1½ cups Shrimp Curry	645	• 1 cup Chicken Curry	923	• 1 cup Sweet and Sour Chicken	527
• 2 cups Fried Rice	876	• 2 cups Vegetable Fried Rice	416	• 1½ cups Pad Jay (mixed vegetables with Thai spices)	225
• 1 cup Coconut Ice Cream	1,091	• 1 cup Coconut Ice Cream	1,091	• 2 cups Vegetable Fried Rice	416
		• 1 cup Pineapple Chunks	222	• 1 cup Pineapple chunks	222

Total ounces: 34
Total calories of meal: 1,520
Caloric density of meal: 702

Total ounces: 38
Total calories of meal: 1,168
Caloric density of meal: 491

Total ounces: 49
Total calories of meal: 896
Caloric density of meal: 296

Thai Dish 3

AS ORDERED	CD	SLIGHT SUBSTITUTION	CD	MAJOR SUBSTITUTION	CD
• 3 Satay portions	1,104	• 3 Satay portions	1,104	• 2 cups Green Salad	105
½ cup peanut sauce	925			4 Tbsp. lemon juice	113
• 1½ cups Pad Thai	821	• 2 cups Green Salad	150	• Vegetable Stir-Fry	
		1 Tbsp. tamarind	1,080	with Tofu	
		paste		-1½ cups mixed	
				vegetables	267
				-1 cup tofu	349
				-2 Tbsp. teriyaki	381
				sauce	
• 2 cups	754	• 1½ cups Pad Thai	821	• 1½ cups mixed	267
Chicken Fried Rice				vegetables	
• 2 items Fried Banana	1,136	• 2 cups	416	• 1 cup Steamed Rice	517
		Vegetable Fried Rice			
		• ½ cup Lychee Nuts	299	• 1 cup Orange Slices	213

Total ounces: 28	Total ounces: 37	Total ounces: 41
Total calories of meal: 1,669	Total calories of meal: 1,182	Total calories of meal: 720
Caloric density of meal: 953	**Caloric density of meal: 500**	**Caloric density of meal: 284**

Total ounces, total calories, and caloric density (CD) do not include liquids.

THE CALORIE DENSITY INDEX

The caloric density of common foods is provided in this chapter. The index is arranged in food groups—Beans, Peas, and Lentils, is one group, Candy is another, Cereals still another. The groups are arranged alphabetically. There are 21 food groups, everything from Cheese and Cheese Products to Vegetables. Within each food group are that group's common foods. For example, within the Beans, Peas, and Lentils group, you will find the common dried beans, such as black and pinto, as well as the common prepared bean products, such as baked beans and split peas cooked with fat.

The index provides the calorie density for unprocessed foods, such as those typically bought in bulk, as well as for common processed foods. You'll find, for example, the calorie density for Cheerios (1,780 calories per pound) under Cereals; Hostess Snack Cakes (1,710) under Desserts, and Gloria's Kitchen's Jamaican Jerk Tofu with Vegetables and Rice (450 calories per pound) under Frozen Meals.

I recommend that you peruse the entire Index to get a feeling for the calorie densities of different foods. It's very illuminating and sometimes a bit disillusioning. For example, that old "healthful standby," the corn muffin, has a calorie density of 1,430 calories per pound—you can find it under Desserts—while those innocent-looking bagel chips have a calorie density of 1,930 calories per pound. Compare these with the food that's always had the scarlet letter emblazed on it, the sinful cheese-filled blintz, which weighs in at a relatively modest 890 calories per pound.

As a general rule of thumb, I always question foods that are labeled "fat-free," such as the Entenmann's fat-free Cookies, which have a calorie density of 1,510 calories per pound, or Health Valley's fat-free cookies, which have a calorie density of 1,270 calories per pound. The cookies may be fat-free, but the odds are that you won't be after you eat them.

I like to question things that are marked "dietetic," too, such as those "dietetic cookies," which have a calorie density of 2,180. They're not going to be good for anyone who considers herself a "dietetic" or anyone who may be a "diabetic."

Beware of foods with sentence-long names, too, such as "I Can't Believe It's Not Butter!" Sweet Cream Buttermilk Squeeze. It's got a calorie density of 2,920 calories per pound. Weight Watchers Light Margarine isn't very light at 1,460 calories per pound.

On the other hand, there are a lot of foods that are moderate to very low in calorie density, some of which may surprise you. Check out all the grains, vegetables, beans, and fruit. But also see the Bumble Bee and Starkist tunas, both packed in water, with a calorie density of 490. (Beware the standard mayonnaise, of course, which has a calorie density of 3,250. Kraft makes a fat-free mayonnaise dressing that's only 285 calories per pound, however.) Wolfgang Puck's got a fat-free Cheeseless Pizza with a calorie density of 590, and Amy has a Tomato and Spinach Pizza that's also got a calorie density of 590 calories per pound.

Always keep in mind that calorie density is not the only guide when measuring the value of a particular food. There are many low-calorie dense foods that will cause weight loss but will increase your risk of disease. You want to eat foods that reduce your weight *and* promote good health. We at the Pritikin Longevity Center have created an eating plan that is both health-promoting and low in calorie density. For this reason, we recommend that you maintain consistency on the Pritikin Program. And when you deviate, use the calorie density principles to lower the weight-producing effects of foods.

Anyway, you get the idea. Go over the Index carefully and let it teach you how you can regain your healthy weight, look great, and enjoy life as you do it.

CALORIC DENSITY INDEX

Beans, Peas, and Lentils	Calorie Density
Beans, baked, prepared	680
Beans, black, boiled	600
Beans, fava, boiled	730
Beans, garbanzo (chickpeas), boiled	740
Beans, pink, boiled	680
Beans, pinto, boiled	620
Beans, lima, boiled	560
Beans, pinto, boiled	510
Beans, pinto, calico, or Red Mexican, cooked with fat	740
Beans, red kidney, boiled	580
Beans, white, boiled	630
Lentils, boiled	530
Lima beans and corn (succotash), cooked	520
Peas, black-eyed, boiled	530
Peas, creamed	530
Peas, green or yellow split, cooked	550
Peas, green, boiled and drained	380
Peas, green, canned and drained	310
Peas, split, cooked without fat	540
Peas and carrots, cooked with fat	300
Peas and carrots, cooked without fat	220
Peas and corn, cooked with fat	520
Peas and corn, cooked without fat	430
Peas and onions, cooked with fat	290
Peas and onions, cooked without fat	200
Soybeans*, boiled	780

*For soy products, see pages 119-121.

Candy	Calorie Density
Butterfinger	2,130
Caramel	1,810
Chocolate bar, Hershey's plain	2,360
Chocolate with almonds, Nestle's Alpine White	2,450
Chocolate fudge	1,820
Gumdrops	1,750
Jelly beans	1,670
Kit Kat	2,290
Licorice	1,670
M & M's Peanut Chocolate Candies	2,310
M & M's Plain Chocolate Candies	2,270
Peanut brittle	2,050
Reese's Peanut Butter Cup	2,450
Reese's Pieces	2,180
Rolos	2,250
Snickers	2,160
Three Musketeers Bar	1,950
Tootsie Roll	1,780
Twix Peanut Butter Cookie Bar	2,780

Cereals	Calorie Density
Ready-to-eat cereals:	
All Bran	1,130
Apple Jacks	1,760
Bran flakes, Kellogg's 40%	1,480
Cap'n Crunch	1,910
Cheerios	1,780
Cornflakes, Kellogg's	1,770
Cocoa Krispies	1,760
Granola	2,210

Cereals *continued*	Calorie Density
Granola with cinnamon and raisins, Nature Valley	2,070
Granola, Honey Crunch, Health Valley	1,760
Grape-Nuts	1,640
Product 19	1,730
Puffed Kashi	1,270
Raisin Bran, Post	1,390
Rice Krispies	1,790
Shredded Wheat	1,610
Smart Start, Kellogg's	1,630
Cooked cereals:	
Farina	240
Grits	270
Kashi	550
Oat bran	260
Oat and hot grain	320
Oatmeal	280
Wheat and barley	230
Whole wheat, Ralston 100% wheat	270

Cheese and Cheese Products	Calorie Density
American, regular	1,700
American, Healthy Choice white American singles	650
American, Kraft Free singles nonfat	720
American, Smart Beat fat-free	600
American, Weight Watchers reduced-sodium	640
Cheddar, regular	1,820
Cheddar, Dormans, low sodium, low-fat	1,280
Cheddar, Alpine Lace fat-free	720
Cheddar, Nu Tofu fat-free cheddar flavored cheese alternative	640
Cottage cheese, 2% fat	410

Cheese and Cheese Products *continued*	Calorie Density
Cottage cheese, Knudsen fat-free	300
Cottage cheese, Lucerne 1% fat	320
Cottage cheese, Lucerne fat-free	280
Cream cheese, fat-free	430
Cream cheese, regular	1,580
Cream cheese, Healthy Choice plain	380
Cream cheese, Philadelphia Light soft	990
Cream cheese, Tofutti better than cream cheese	1,280
Mozzarella cheese, whole milk	1,270
Mozzarella cheese, part skim	1,150
Mozzarella cheese, Alpine Lace fat-free	720
Mozzarella cheese, Nu Tofu fat-free cheese alternative	640
Ricotta cheese, Frigo fat-free	350
Ricotta cheese, Frigo low-fat	470
Ricotta cheese, Gardenia low-fat	470
Ricotta cheese, part skim milk	630
Ricotta cheese, Sargento light	440
Ricotta cheese, Sargento Old-Fashioned	660
Ricotta cheese, Sargento part skim ricotta cheese	590
Ricotta cheese, whole milk	790
Swiss, regular	1,700
Swiss, Kraft Swiss Singles process cheese food slices, ⅓ less fat	1,080
Swiss, Pauly County Line Advantage, low-sodium, low-fat	1,280
Swiss, Weight Watchers fat-free	640

Chips, Pretzels, Popcorn, and Similar Snack Foods	Calorie Density
Bagel chips	1,930
Cheese puffs, Health Valley	1,660
Chex Mix, traditional	1,970

Chips, Pretzels, Popcorn, and Similar Snack Foods *continued*	Calorie Density
Corn chips	2,450
Corn puffs and twists	2,470
Goldfish Snacks	2,120
Melba toast	1,770
Popcorn, plain	1,730
Popcorn, with oil and salt	2,270
Popcorn, Healthy Choice Natural Microwave Popcorn	1,510
Popcorn, low-fat	1,860
Potato chips	2,400
Potato chips, Louise's fat-free baked	1,760
Potato chips, WOW! fat-free	1,220
Pretzels	1,770
Pretzels, Louise's fat-free sourdough	1,440
Pretzels, Rold Gold Tiny Twist	1,600
Pretzels, Rold Gold fat-free sourdough	1,300
Pretzels, Super Pretzel All Natural Soft	1,210
Pringle's Original Potato Crisps	2,550
Pringle's Right Crisps Original Potato Crisps	2,240
Rice cakes	1,750
Tortilla chips, Doritos Nacho Cheesier	2,240
Tortilla chips, Tostitos	2,400
Tortilla chips, light	2,100
Tortilla chips, Louise's 95% fat-free	1,920

Cream and Cream Substitutes	Calorie Density
Sour cream, regular	970
Sour cream, reduced-fat	610
Sour cream, Knudsen Light	590
Sour cream, Knudsen fat-free	490
Sour cream, Land O' Lakes fat-free	425

Desserts	Calorie Density
Brownies and other bar cookies:	
Brownie, regular	1,720
Brownie, Entenmann's fat-free	1,250
Fig Newton	1,630
Granola bar, Barbara's Bakery peanut butter	1,730
Granola bar, hard	2,140
Granola bar, soft	2,000
Granola bar, peanut butter, milk chocolate coated, soft	2,300
Granola bar, Health Valley fat-free	1,500
Cakes:	
Angel food cake	1,170
Apple spice crumb cake, Entenmann's fat-free, cholesterol-free	1,180
Applesauce cake	1,670
Banana cake	1,300
Butter pound cake	1,760
Carrot cake	1,850
Chiffon cake	1,560
Cheesecake, regular	1,440
Cheesecake, chocolate	1,770
Chocolate fudge cake	1,690
Coffeecake	1,440
Dobos Torte cake (including seven-layer cake)	1,840
Entenmann's cake, fat-free	1,120
Fruit cake	1,740
German chocolate cake	1,700
Sponge cake	1,380
Spice cake	1,490
Cupcakes and snack cakes:	
Chocolate cupcakes	1,550
Hostess Snack Cakes orange cupcakes	1,710
Cookies:	
Chocolate chip cookies	2,140

Desserts *continued*	**Calorie Density**
Dietetic cookies	2,180
Entenmann's fat-free cookies	1,510
Health Valley fat-free cookies	1,270
Oreos	2,200
Peanut butter cookies	2,290
Peanut butter sandwich cookies	2,170
Peanut butter chocolate chip, Grandma's Big Cookies	2,210
Snackwell's Cookie Cakes	1,420
Windmill, almond or traditional spice	1,740
Muffins:	
Banana oat bran muffin, Hostess low-fat	1,180
Blueberry muffin	1,260
Blueberry muffin, Entenmann's fat-free, cholesterol-free	960
Chocolate chip mini muffin, Hostess Snack Cakes	2,130
Corn muffin	1,430
Multigrain muffin with nuts	1,440
Oat bran muffin	1,210
Pastries:	
Pastry puff (including angel wings, flaky pastry)	2,360
Pastry, Entenmann's fat-free	1,200
Éclair, custard filled, with chocolate glaze	1,190
Empanada, fruit-filled pastry	1,890
Pies:	
Apple pie	1,380
Apple or cherry beehive pie, Entenmann's fat-free	940
Banana cream pie	1,140
Blueberry pie	1,050
Cherry pie	1,220
Coconut custard pie	1,180
Lemon meringue pie	1,290
Pumpkin pie	970

Desserts *continued*	Calorie Density
Miscellaneous:	
Apple cobbler	980
Baklava	1,940
Biscotti	2,150
Blintz, cheese-filled	890
Blintz, fruit-filled	800
Churros	2,010
Croissants, butter	1,840
Cruller	1,780
Doughnut	1,830
Raspberry cheese bun, Entenmann's fat-free	1,100
Strudel, apple	1,240
Zabaglione	1,190

Fats, Oils, and Shortenings	Calorie Density
Animal fats:	
Bacon grease or meat drippings	4,100
Butter, regular	3,250
Butter, Land O' Lakes light	1,620
Ghee, clarified butter	3,980
Lard	4,100
Margarine and shortenings:	
Brummel and Brown spread	1,460
"I Can't Believe It's Not Butter!" Sweet Cream Buttermilk Squeeze	2,920
"I Can't Believe It's Not Butter!" Light Spread, 40% Vegetable Oil	1,620
Margarine, soft	3,250
Margarine, whipped	3,250
Margarine, Weight Watchers light	1,460
Shortening	4,020

Fats, Oils, and Shortenings *continued*	Calorie Density
Miscellaneous:	
Oil, all varieties	4,010

Fish, Shellfish, and Crustacea	Calorie Density
Clams, baked	630
Clams, breaded and fried	830
Clams, moist heat, steamed	670
Clams, smoked, in soybean oil, Crown Prince	870
Cod, cooked	480
Crab, cooked	460
Crab, King, cooked	460
Crab, soft shell, breaded and fried	1,520
Fish sticks, battered and fried	940
Halibut, battered and baked	810
Halibut, broiled in butter	780
Halibut, cooked, dry heat	640
Halibut, poached	520
Halibut, sautéed, no coating	610
Herring, pickled	1,190
Lobster, boiled	450
Orange roughy, cooked, dry heat	400
Oysters, smoked, in cottonseed oil, Crown Prince	910
Oysters, smoked, in cottonseed oil, Geisha	1,090
Salmon, canned with bones	620
Salmon, cooked, dry heat	680
Salmon, Coho, farmed, cooked, dry heat	810
Salmon, poached	660
Salmon, sautéed	780
Sardines, in olive oil, Tiny Tots	920
Sardines, in soybean oil, Crown Prince	1,280

Fish, Shellfish, and Crustacea *continued*	Calorie Density
Sardines, in tomato sauce, Crown Prince	770
Scallops, baked or broiled	600
Scallops, battered and fried	1,050
Shrimp, breaded and fried	1,120
Shrimp, boiled	630
Tuna, bluefin, cooked	830
Tuna, canned, oil packed, Bumble Bee and Starkist	890
Tuna, canned, water packed, Bumble Bee and Starkist	490

Frozen Meals	Calorie Density
Beef and gravy dinner, Swanson	530
Beef Pepper Steak Oriental Entrée, Healthy Choice	420
Beef sirloin salisbury steak entrée, Budget Gourmet	430
Cheese Ravioli Entrée, Stouffer's Lean Cuisine	450
Chicken a la King dinner, Stouffer's	640
Chicken Broccoli Alfredo Dinner, Healthy Choice	490
Chicken Chow Mein with Rice Entrée, Stouffer's Lean Cuisine	370
Chicken Fettuccine Entrée, Stouffer's Lean Cuisine	480
Chicken Free Nuggets, Health is Wealth	650
Chicken nuggets dinner, Swanson	990
Chicken Pie Entrée, Stouffer's Lean Cuisine	540
Chicken with Fettuccine entrée, Budget Gourmet	610
Chopped sirloin beef with gravy dinner, Swanson	570
Country Glazed Chicken Entrée, Healthy Choice	380
Enchilada, Bean and Corn with Cheese, Amy's	590
Enchilada, Black Bean Vegetable, Amy's	380
Enchilada, Garden Vegetable, Cedarlane	480
Enchilada, Vegetarian, Cascadian Farms	590
Fettuccine Alfredo entrée, Stouffer's	930
Fish and chips entrée, Stouffer's	860

Frozen Meals *continued*	**Calorie Density**
Fried chicken dinner, Swanson	970
Jamaican Jerk Tofu with Vegetables & Rice, Gloria's Kitchen	450
Lasagna Roma Entrée, Healthy Choice	460
Lasagna with meat sauce casserole, Swanson	520
Lasagna three cheese entrée, Budget Gourmet	560
Lasagna vegetable entrée, Budget Gourmet	440
Lasagna, Tofu Vegetable, Amy's	500
Linguine with shrimp and clams entrée, Budget Gourmet	470
Macaroni and Cheese, Healthy Choice	520
Macaroni and Cheese Entrée, Stouffer's	880
Macaroni and Cheese, Stouffer's Lean Cuisine	480
Meatloaf dinner, Swanson	540
Mexican style combination dinner, Swanson	570
Salisbury steak with macaroni and cheese, Stouffer's Lean Cuisine	460
Salisbury steak dinner, Swanson	470
Salisbury steak in gravy with mashed potato entrée, Swanson	530
Sirloin beef tips with noodles and beef gravy dinner, Swanson	660
Spaghetti and meatballs entrée, Stouffer's	530
Spinach Tofu Munchies, Health is Wealth	860
Sweet and sour chicken entrée, Budget Gourmet	530
Three Cheese Manicotti Entrée, Healthy Choice	450
Tofu Balls with Spaghetti, Gloria's Kitchen	480
Turkey dinner, Swanson	440
Turkey tetrazzini entrée, Stouffer's	570
Veal parmigiana dinner, Swanson	610
Veggie Bowl Teriyaki Rice, Cascadian Farms	480

Fruits	**Calorie Density**
Dried:	
Apple	1,100

Fruits *continued*	Calorie Density
Apricot	1,080
Cranberries	1,470
Currants	1,280
Dates	1,250
Fig	1,160
Lychee	1,260
Papaya	1,170
Peach	1,090
Pineapple	1,140
Prune	1,090
Raisins	1,360
Fresh:	
Apple	270
Apricot	220
Avocado	800
Banana	420
Berries	140
Blueberries	250
Cantaloupe	140
Cherries	330
Currants	250
Fig	340
Grapefruit	150
Grapes	300
Guava	230
Kiwi	280
Lychee	300
Mango	300
Nectarines	220
Olive, green or black	520
Oranges	210
Papaya	180

Fruits *continued*	**Calorie Density**
Peach	200
Pear	270
Pineapple	220
Raspberry	220
Strawberry	140
Watermelon	150

Grain Products	**Calorie Density**
Biscuits:	
Cheese biscuits	1,740
Drop biscuits	1,270
Wheat biscuits	1,360
Breads:	
Bagel, plain	1,270
Bagel, whole wheat	1,260
Bagel, toasted	1,360
Bread, dough, fried	1,680
Cornbread	1,120
Egg bread (Challah)	1,470
English muffin, sourdough	1,030
English muffin, plain	1,070
English muffin, whole wheat	920
Italian bread	1,230
Italian bread, Wonder Light reduced calorie	810
Pannetone (Italian-style sweetbread)	1,450
Pita bread	1,250
Pita bread, white, Thomas'	1,190
Pita bread, 100% whole wheat, Thomas'	1,110
Pumpernickel bread	1,130
Pumpernickel bread, toasted	1,250

Grain Products *continued*	Calorie Density
Roll, sourdough	1,320
Rye bread, regular	1,190
Rye bread, reduced-calorie, high-fiber	920
Rye bread, toasted	1,290
Scone, regular	1,620
Scone, Health Valley fat-free	1,360
Sourdough bread	1,240
Sourdough bread, Wonder Light reduced-calorie	810
Sprouted wheat bread	1,190
White bread	1,210
White bread, low-calorie, high-fiber, toasted	1,030
White bread, reduced-calorie	940
White bread, toasted	1,330
White bread, Wonder	1,130
White bread, Wonder Light reduced-calorie	810
Whole-wheat bread	1,280
Whole-wheat bread, 100% whole wheat	1,240
Breadsticks:	
Breadstick, soft	1,610
Breadstick, sesame stick	1,930
Crackers:	
Brown rice snaps, Edward & Sons	1,810
Brown rice wafers, Westbrae Natural	1,510
Crackers, butter	2,280
Crackers, cheese	2,170
Crackers, Health Valley fat-free whole-wheat	1,620
Crackers, Health Valley, fat-free whole-wheat herb	800
Crackers, Health Valley, fat-free whole-wheat vegetable	1,620
Crackers, graham	1,740
Crackers, Health Valley, fat-free graham amaranth	1,570
Crackers, Keebler Zesta fat-free saltines	1,620
Crackers, Matzo	1,810

Grain Products *continued*	Calorie Density
Crackers, oyster	1,990
Crackers, Premium fat-free	1,620
Crackers, rye crisp bread	1,660
Crackers, saltine	1,970
Crackers, Snackwell's reduced-fat cheese	1,970
Crackers, Snackwell's reduced-fat classic golden	1,950
Crackers, Snackwell's reduced-fat cracked pepper	1,820
Crackers, Snackwell's fat-free wheat	1,810
Crackers, Sunshine Krispy	1,810
Crackers, Triscuit	1,820
Pastas:	
Corn pasta, cooked	570
Dried pasta, cooked	630
Homemade pasta, cooked	560
Homemade pasta with egg, cooked	590
Noodles, egg, cooked	600
Noodles, spinach egg, cooked	600
Plain pasta, fresh-refrigerated, cooked	595
Spinach pasta, cooked	590
Whole-wheat pasta, cooked	560
Rice:	
Rice, brown, cooked	500
Rice, brown, wild, cooked	460
Rice, white, cooked	580
Tortillas and tostadas:	
Taco shell	2,060
Taco shell, Mission	2,270
Tortilla, corn	1,000
Tortilla, flour	1,470
Tortilla, wheat, Guerrero	1,510
Tortilla, wheat, 96% fat-free, Mission	1,250
Tostada crowns, Del Oro	1,970

Grain Products *continued*	Calorie Density
Tostada, Guerrero	2,270
Miscellaneous:	
Buckwheat groats (including kasha), cooked	420
Bulgur, cooked	380
Cous Cous, cooked	510

Meat	Calorie Density
Beef:	
Beef brisket	1,550
Corned beef	1,140
Eye of round	820
Ground beef, extra-lean, broiled medium	1,130
Ground beef, lean, broiled medium	1,235
Ground beef, regular, broiled medium	1,310
Pastrami	1,580
Porterhouse steak	1,390
Rib eye, "choice," separable lean, $^1/_4$-inch fat, broiled	1,020
Round, "prime"	975
Short ribs	2,150
Top round, separable lean and fat, $^1/_4$-inch fat, broiled	980
Top round, separable lean and fat, 0-inch fat, braised	950
Top sirloin	870
Game meat:	
Antelope	670
Beefalo	860
Deer	720
Venison	770
Water Buffalo	600
Wild Boar	730
Wild Rabbit	790

Meat *continued*	Calorie Density
Lamb:	
Lamb steak	1,620
Leg of lamb	1,270
Bacon	2,170
Canadian bacon	840
Ham	780
Pork:	
Pork chops	1,560
Pork tenderloin	750
Spareribs	1,790
Veal:	
Veal chop	1,060
Veal cutlet	980
Veal cutlet, breaded and fried	1,120
Other meats:	
Bologna	1,440
Hot dog	1,500
Knockwurst	1,400
Pepperoni	2,260
Sausage, Healthy Choice breakfast patties	500
Sausage, Italian	1,470
Sausage, Polish	1,410
Sausage links, brown and serve	1,430
(Calorie densities are for cooked meat.)	

Nuts, Nut Products, and Seeds	Calorie Density
Almonds	2,670
Brazil nuts	2,980
Cashews	2,610
Chestnuts	1,110

Nuts, Nut Products, and Seeds *continued*	Calorie Density
Coconuts	2,990
Filberts, hazel nuts	2,870
Flaxseeds	2,260
Macadamia nuts	3,260
Mixed nuts	2,800
Peanuts	2,640
Peanut butter, chunky	2,670
Peanut butter, natural	2,610
Peanut butter, smooth	2,670
Peanut butter, old-fashioned	2,690
Peanut butter, Better n' Peanut Butter 85% less fat	1,420
Peanut butter, Skippy Super Chunk	2,690
Peanut butter, Skippy Super Chunk, reduced-fat	2,330
Peanut butter, Fifty 50 no added sugar	2,850
Pecans	3,030
Pine nuts (Pignolias)	2,340
Pumpkin seeds	2,370
Soy nuts	2,110
Sunflower seeds	2,640
Trail Mix	2,100
Walnuts	2,910

Pizza	Calorie Density
Cheeseless Grilled Vegetable Pizza, Wolfgang Puck's fat-free	590
French Bread Pizza, cheese, Stouffer's	1,080
French Bread Pizza, cheese, Stouffer's Lean Cuisine	940
French Bread Pizza, sausage and pepperoni, Stouffer's	1,260
Mushroom Spinach Pizza, Wolfgang Puck's	840
Pepperoni French Bread Pizza, Healthy Choice	860
Pizza with cheese, thin crust	1,010

Pizza *continued*	Calorie Density
Pizza with cheese, thick crust	1,290
Pizza, combination with meat and vegetables	1,060
Pizza, combination supreme	810
Pizza with chicken, mushrooms, and tomatoes	970
Pizza with chicken and pineapple	1,290
Pizza with meat, thick crust	1,400
Pizza with meat and vegetables, thick crust	1,220
Pizza with meat and vegetables, thin crust	1,110
Pizza with onion, tomato, green pepper, and mushroom	730
Pizza with pepperoni	1,160
Roasted Vegetable Pizza, Bravissimo	790
Soy Cheese Pizza, Amy's	1,030
Tomato and Spinach Pizza, Amy's	590
Vegetable Deluxe French Bread Pizza, Stouffer's	1,000

Poultry	Calorie Density
Chicken:	
Chicken breast, breaded, baked, or fried with skin	1,060
Chicken breast, breaded, baked, or fried without skin	840
Chicken breast, broiled with skin	890
Chicken breast, broiled without skin	750
Chicken leg, breaded, baked, or fried with skin	1,190
Chicken leg, broiled with skin	1,040
Chicken leg, breaded, baked, or fried without skin	930
Chicken leg, broiled without skin	860
Chicken liver	710
Chicken nuggets	1,340
Chicken nuggets, McDonalds	1,170
Turkey:	
Breast loaf	500

Poultry *continued*	Calorie Density
Dark meat, roasted with skin	1,000
Dark meat, roasted without skin	840
Ground turkey, cooked	1,070
Ground turkey, Louis Rich	780
Ground turkey, Mr. Turkey, 91% fat-free	680
Light meat, roasted with skin	890
Light meat, roasted without skin	710
Turkey ham	640
Turkey salami	890
Turkey pastrami	640
Miscellaneous:	
Cornish game hen, with skin	1,080
Cornish game hen, without skin	860
Duck, roasted with skin	1,520
Duck, roasted without skin	910
Goose, roasted	1,080

Salad Dressings	Calorie Density
Low-calorie and/or reduced-fat salad dressings:	
Blue cheese dressing, low-calorie	450
Catalina dressing, Kraft Free, fat-free	480
French dressing, low-fat	610
Honey Dijon dressing, Weight Watchers fat-free	680
Italian dressing, Kraft Free, fat-free	270
Mayonnaise type dressing, reduced-fat	1,310
Russian dressing, low-fat	640
Ranch dressing, Seven Seas Free, fat-free	580
Regular salad dressings:	
Blue or Roquefort cheese dressing	2,290
Caesar dressing	2,400

Salad Dressings *continued*	Calorie Density
French dressing	1,950
Italian dressing	2,120
Mayonnaise type dressing >35% oil	2,250
Oil and vinegar	2,040
Thousand Island dressing	1,710

Sauces, Condiments, Spreads, and Dips	Calorie Density
Bean dip, made with refried beans	630
Guacamole, California style, Fresh Scotty's	480
Hollandaise sauce	2,510
Horseradish sauce, Heinz	2,270
Hummus, basil and sundried tomato, Cedarlane	810
Hummus, roasted pepper and olive, Meza	1,130
Hummus, spicy, Meza	810
Mayonnaise, regular	3,250
Mayonnaise, imitation, low-calorie, or diet	1,050
Mayonnaise, Kraft Fat-Free Mayonnaise dressing	285
Nacho cheese dip, Kaukauna	1,360
Pesto sauce	2,430

Soy Products	Calorie Density
Cheese:	
Cheese, Nu Tofu fat-free cheddar flavored cheese alternative	640
Cheese, Nu Tofu cheddar flavored cheese alternative	1,120
Cheese, Nu Tofu fat-free Monterey Jack cheese alternative	640
Cheese, Nu Tofu Monterey Jack flavored cheese alternative	1,120
Cheese, Nu Tofu fat-free mozzarella cheese alternative	640
Cheese, Nu Tofu low-sodium mozzarella cheese alternative	1,120

119

Soy Products *continued*	Calorie Density
Cream cheese, Tofutti better than cream cheese	1,280
Tempeh:	
Tempeh (fermented soybeans)	720
White Wave Original Soy Tempeh	895
White Wave Soy Rice Tempeh	835
Tofu:	
Tofu, extra firm, silken, Mori-Nu	300
Tofu, firm, Kikkoman	270
Tofu, firm, silken, Mori-Nu	270
Tofu, fried	1,230
Tofu, lite, extra firm, silken, Mori-Nu	190
Tofu, soft, silken, Mori-Nu	240
Tofu, soft, Kikkoman	250
Tofu, White Wave, reduced-fat	450
Convenience Products:	
Amy's Kitchen Macaroni and Soy Cheese	640
Amy's Kitchen Tofu Vegetable Lasagna	510
Boca Burger 98% Fat Free	700
Boca Burger 99% Fat Free	620
Boca Burger 100% Fat Free	540
Boca Breakfast Patties	840
Nature's Hilights Soy Cheese Pizza	840
Miscellaneous:	
Miso (fermented soybean) paste	930
Soybean cake, fried	1,000
Soybean cake, spiced	590
Soybean curd	300
Soybean noodles	1,590
Soybeans, black	1,700
Soybeans, dry roasted	2,040
Soybeans, sprouted, raw	550
Soybeans, sprouted, stir-fry	570

Soy Products *continued*	Calorie Density
Soybeans, white	1,840

Sugars, Syrups, and Other Products	Calorie Density
Honey	1,380
Jam/jelly, regular	1,230
Jam/jelly, reduced-sugar	810
Molasses	1,140
Sugar, brown	1,690
Sugar, cinnamon	1,710
Sugar, granulated	1,730
Sugar, white, confectioner's	1,750
Syrup, cane, corn, maple	1,200
Syrup, reduced-calorie	780

Vegetables	Calorie Density	Calorie Density	Calorie Density
Type	Raw	Cooked without fat	Cooked with fat
Artichoke	215	115	435
Asparagus	100	115	200
Beets	200	140	230
Broccoli	130	130	210
Brussels sprouts	195	180	275
Cabbage, Chinese	60	65	155
Carrots	195	205	305
Cauliflower	110	100	205
Celery Stalks	65	70	190
Chard	85	90	195

Vegetables *continued*	Calorie Density	Calorie Density	Calorie Density
Type	Raw	Cooked without fat	Cooked with fat
Corn	390	490	570
Cucumber	70	75	205
Eggplant	120	130	200
Kale	130	145	280
Mushrooms	115	120	225
Onions	155	130	200
Peppers	115	80	200
Radishes	80	90	190
Spinach	100	105	190
Tomato, red	90	90	170
Tomato, cherry	95	95	175
Turnip greens	90	90	200
Zucchini	65	75	175

Vegetables, Miscellaneous	Calorie Density
Green beans, raw	160
Jicama, raw	190
Lettuce	65
Olives	530
Potato, baked	490
Potato, boiled	390
Potato, fried (French fries)	1,450
Potato, sweet	475
Pumpkin	150
Yams, baked	525

7 | EXERCISE, WEIGHT LOSS, AND HEALTH

Just like us, words can get tired and worn out. They can even lose their meaning. Two words that are extremely tired, to the point that you can hardly hear them without going brain dead or conjuring up lots of inaccurate associations, are the words "sedentary" and "exercise." The American Heritage Dictionary tells us that sedentary means "1. Characterized by or requiring much sitting: a sedentary job. 2. Accustomed to sitting or to taking little exercise. 3. Remaining in one area; not migratory. 4. Zoology. Attached to a surface and not free-moving, as a barnacle." I especially like two of the dictionary's phrases—"much sitting," and "not free-moving, as a barnacle." You can almost see an old Indian chief complaining in his noble way about a long council meeting by saying, "There was much sitting." He'd be speaking volumes with that little phrase. Or an old sea captain grousing about some long-winded gathering by saying, "If we sat any longer, I'd be a barnacle on that chair."

When I think about that word sedentary, and particularly the phrase "much sitting," another word comes to mind: stagnation. The word stagnation conjures up images of being in a rut, of suffering from poor blood circulation, and having the silent killer, heart disease. Sedentary lifestyles and the stagnation that results cause us to slow down physically and mentally. They indicate that the aging process has accelerated, which of course leads to death.

Humans were designed to move their bodies, to promote the circulation of blood and oxygen to every cell in the body. Throughout our evolution and virtually all of human history, we have been very busy physically.

Mostly we walked and lifted and pulled heavy objects. We were migratory people, traveling to places with better weather and greater food supplies. When agriculture arose, we plowed the fields, built houses, tamed wild horses. In other words, we have grown accustomed, biologically speaking, to spending many hours flexing our muscles.

Unfortunately, our current age is characterized by much sitting, stagnation, rapid aging, and much premature death. And many of our problems begin with our lack of physical activity, or exercise.

EXERCISE: A VERY SIMPLE AND EASY PRESCRIPTION

The word exercise has many meanings—the dictionary's definition is more than two inches long—but a couple of them suit our purposes perfectly: "1. An act of employing or putting into play; use. . . . 3. Activity that requires physical or mental exertion, especially when performed to develop or maintain fitness."

Effective exercise need not be any more demanding than simply putting your body into play, as the dictionary says. In short, be active. Being active does not necessarily mean heart-pounding exertion. In order to lose weight and keep it off, all you have to do is walk for two or three miles per day, at a moderate pace, over a 30-to-40 minute period. For more effective weight loss, you would walk 45 minutes a day.

Ideally, you would do all two or three miles in a single exercise session, but research has shown that you will still benefit enormously even if you break up your walking into, say, three 15-minute walking sessions.

GOOD ADVICE: DO WHAT THOSE WHO HAVE LOST WEIGHT DO

For me, the proof of any health program—whether it involves diet or exercise—is in the health of the people who practice it. If those who practice a diet or exercise regimen are lean and healthy, then it's a good bet that the program has value. If we want to know which tools cause sustained weight loss, we should talk to people who were once overweight, or even obese, and now are thin, and ask them how they lost their weight and kept it off. In 1997, researchers did just that. The study, called the National Weight Registry Survey, turned out to be the largest review of its kind.

Mary Lou Klem, Ph.D., of the University of Pittsburgh, and her colleagues gathered information from more than 800 men and women who had achieved significant weight loss and kept that weight off for more than five years. The average weight loss overall was 66 pounds, but many of the people in the study had been significantly obese and some had lost more than

200 pounds. The researchers examined these people's lifestyles to discover what tools they had used to take off their excess weight and keep it off.

Dr. Klem and her colleagues found six surprising facts. The first was that only a tiny percentage of the people were able to lose weight and keep it off by using either diet or exercise alone. Only 10 percent were able to use diet alone to lose weight and only one percent had lost the weight and kept it off by using exercise alone.

The second conclusion that emerged from the study was that the most effective diet for long-term weight loss was one that was low in fat. On average, those who lost weight followed a diet that derived only 23 percent of its calories from fat. About one-third of the people in the study ate a diet that derived less than 20 percent of its calories from fat.

The third observation—and this was crucial—was that these people did a lot of walking. On average, the men walked 30 miles a week, or an average of about four miles per day, while the women walked an average of 26 miles per week, or just under four miles per day. All of us should use that 30-miles-a-week as a goal. However, it's important to keep in mind that a lot of these people were significantly obese. Many had been obese since childhood, which probably meant that they had a genetic predisposition to the disorder. Not everyone who wants to lose weight necessarily falls into that category, which means that four miles per day, though ideal, may not be necessary for people who do not have to lose 150 pounds or more. Some observers have said that people can do slightly less walking— say, two or three miles per day—and compensate by reducing the calorie density of their diets. One way to do this is by eating even less fat than the people in the study already did.

The fourth observation was that those who lost weight and kept it off ate five meals per day—three substantial meals and two snacks between meals. As I have said in previous chapters, this is one of the keys to weight loss, especially if your meals and snacks are low in calorie density.

The fifth conclusion was that these successful people were, in fact, eating a diet low in calorie density. After analyzing the participants' diets, scientists found that their intake of micronutrients from fruits and vegetables was extraordinarily high, which meant that their diets were especially rich in such foods. Fruits and vegetables, as I have been saying, are among the foods lowest in calorie density. Somehow, through trial and error, these people had discovered the Calorie Density Solution, in many cases without even knowing it. (As a small aside that affirms this fact, the majority of these people said they avoided fast-food restaurants, where of course the foods are notoriously high in calorie density.)

Finally, the researchers found no evidence to show that these successful people had lost the weight and kept it off by following a low-carbohydrate, high-protein diet.

As I started out saying, if you want to know what works, ask those who have been successful what they have done to lose weight and keep their weight off. The National Weight Registry Survey provided the ultimate answer to that question.

ONE OF THE SECRET BENEFITS OF EXERCISE: INSULIN EFFICIENCY

Numerous studies have shown that exercise, especially daily walking, is a strong predictor for weight loss. People who exercise regularly have a greater chance of losing weight and keeping it off than those who do not exercise. Yet, the irony is that at 100 calories per mile, exercise does not burn all that many calories. Certainly, the calorie burn is a contributor, but not a great one. Why then is walking such a powerful indicator for sustained weight loss? One reason is that exercise causes your muscles to store sugars and burn fat for many hours after you've stopped exercising. It works like this.

Let's say that you just ate a snack that contains a significant amount of concentrated and rapidly absorbed carbohydrates—a couple of pastries or a few handfuls of pretzels, for example. Once you eat such foods, your blood will likely be flooded with sugars. Your body responds to the elevated quantity of sugars in two ways: by storing them in your muscles and burning them as fuel.

Normally, the fuel your cells burn is composed of a mixture of both fat and sugar—about 50 percent of each. When you eat foods that provide a lot of rapidly absorbed carbs, the sugars that flood your blood force your body to alter the fuel mix. Suddenly, with the rush of sugars, the body turns off its fat-burning and instead burns virtually all sugar as its fuel. The fat that is already in your bloodstream is stored in your fat cells. Any fat that enters your system via your meal is also stored in your fat cells. Obviously, this increases the likelihood that you will gain weight.

But there is a way to keep your body burning fat. The way to do that is by storing the sudden flood of excess carbohydrates in your muscles. This keeps you from having to alter your fuel mix, which means that your cells will go right on burning fat and sugar.

Your capacity to store excess sugar in your muscles depends a great deal on whether or not you exercised on the same day you ate those rapidly absorbed carbs. Exercise causes you to burn sugars stored in your muscles. As your muscles empty, their capacity to store sugar is increased. The more sugars that are stored, the fewer that must be burned as fuel immediately after a meal.

However, if you did not exercise and your muscles are already loaded with sugars, your body will be forced to burn more sugat and less fat. The higher the blood sugar levels, the higher the insulin levels will be in your bood. High insulin levels act as a storage hormone for fat. The higher the insulin levels, the more fat is stored.

Exercise, on the other hand, mobilizes fat from the cells and burns it as fuel. But long after your exercise session is concluded, your relatively empty muscles promote fat-burning for hours. In fact, research has shown that 45 minutes of walking on a treadmill will keep fat-burning high for as much as 20 hours after your exercise session.

When exercise is combined with a diet made up primarily of foods low in calorie density, the combination promotes healthy and effective weight loss.

WALK EVERY DAY TO CREATE STORAGE IN YOUR MUSCLES

One of the keys to weight loss, therefore, is to empty your muscles every day to promote fat-burning. The best way to do this, of course, is to exercise daily. Follow the walking prescription I gave above. In addition, consider doing some weight or resistance training in order to make your muscles as big as possible. Big muscles mean big storage tanks.

Everyone who has ever dieted has lost some muscle mass during the course of their weight loss. In addition, everyone over 40 also loses muscle as a normal course of aging if they do not do some form of resistance training. The more weight we lose and the older we get, therefore, the more we should concentrate on maintaining muscle. For that, I recommend some type of weight or resistance training twice a week. In addition to building muscle and creating bigger storage tanks, resistance training lowers insulin levels.

Weight training can be as simple as doing a few exercises with 5- or 10-pound barbells; you should increase the weight you use as your muscles become more fit. Hand-weights can be held while walking, as well.

STRETCH AND PLAY

After your walking or resistance training, be sure to stretch for 10 to 15 minutes to cool the body, keep muscles from cramping, and reduce the risk of injuries. In addition to walking, resistance training, and stretching, we should all consider having some kind of physical activity that we do for the pure enjoyment and love of the game. Golf, tennis, swimming, racquetball, bicycle riding, cross-country skiing, dancing, basketball, soccer, ice skating, yoga, t'ai chi chuan, martial arts—the list of potential fun-filled sports and activities is long and varied. Fall in love with an activity that forces you to practice and develop your skill. You will find the rewards are endless. Not only will you get a workout, but you'll enjoy every minute of your activity.

THE THREE KEYS TO WEIGHT LOSS

In the end, the formula for weight loss is actually very simple. It includes just three factors:

1. A low-calorie dense diet.

2. Daily exercise.

3. Frequent eating of low-calorie dense meals and snacks. Try to have as many as three low-calorie dense meals and two low-calorie dense snacks each day. This will keep your hunger down and your fat-burning high. As the National Weight Registry Survey demonstrates, these are the keys to long-term weight loss. In fact, as that study demonstrates, these are perhaps the only tools that work.

BOB SINGER'S STORY

Bob Singer had all his dreams for success and wealth come true, but at the relatively young age of 45, he did not have the health to enjoy a single bit of his success. Bob owned a franchise chain of 250 fast-food restaurants. Unfortunately, the travel to new openings and the food associated with his business were killing him. At five feet nine inches tall, Bob weighed more than 200 pounds and was more than 60 pounds overweight. His blood cholesterol level was 350 mg/dl. He had dangerously high blood pressure, gout, and insomnia. "My legs were horribly swollen," he said. "I was miserable, totally miserable. I was nervous, I couldn't sleep at night, but in the morning I couldn't wake myself up." His doctor told him flatly that he did not have many months to live. That was December 1977. Neither Bob nor his doctor believed he would see December 1978.

That December, Bob checked into the Pritikin Longevity Center, arriving in a wheelchair. As Bob recalls, he was prepared for a diet different from the food he was used to eating, but he was not prepared to do anything that resembled exercise. His exercise prescription was to walk around the block on which the center stood, a feat that, when he accomplished it, felt to Bob like a "minor miracle." The next day, he did two revolutions around the block. The following day he did three. Each successive day, he added a revolution until, after 28 days at the Pritikin Center, he was running four miles per day.

Bob's been maintaining the same regimen ever since. Today, his weight is 150 and his cholesterol level is 180 mg/dl. He runs on a treadmill for 45 minutes every weekday and twice a week does one hour of resistance training at his health club. On Saturday and Sunday, he takes long leisurely walks. He assiduously maintains a schedule that permits him to eat three full meals and two snacks per day, even when he is traveling. He begins almost every day with a big bowl of oatmeal with sliced banana or some other fruit; a fruit break at midmorning, and a giant salad at lunch. He takes another fruit or soup break at midafternoon and then dinner with a soup, a wide variety of steamed vegetables, brown rice, barley, or baked potato.

"I eat a lot of whole grains," said Bob. "Every now and then I eat white rice. I usually don't eat animal protein during the week," but on Saturdays he splurges on his barbecue, where he makes a "nice half-pound of salmon" or some other fish.

"That's my big treat day," he says. "I know it's more than what Pritikin recommends, but what the heck, it's once a week." He also drinks half a bottle of well-chosen wine—another extravagance he permits himself. "That's my alcohol quota for the week," said Bob.

Overall, Bob has made the Pritikin Program work for him and he's more than satisfied with the diet, his exercise program, and his results. "My taste buds over the years have adjusted so that now I'm tasting foods as they really do taste without the benefit of salt, sugar and added fat."

"I really do feel that Nathan Pritikin saved my life. . . . I don't think there's any question that if I hadn't gotten on the program I wouldn't be here today. As far as I'm concerned the Pritikin Program is the greatest."

FROM ANCIENT TIMES TO MODERN: A LONG, CONSISTENT PATTERN SUDDENLY INTERRUPTED

One of the great strengths of American culture is that we are always embracing and developing new ideas. We leap into the frontier and come up with creative ways of dealing with our problems. Ironically, this characteristic is also one of our greatest weaknesses. Why? Because we often believe that what is new is better, and thus discard valuable and effective approaches in exchange for some new method that sometimes proves worthless. This observation is hardly new, of course, but few people realize that it applies directly to our problems with obesity and many common illnesses.

The epidemic of overweight and obesity is largely a modern phenomenon. The percentage of Americans who are considered obese—that is, at least 20 percent above their ideal weight—jumped dramatically during the 1980s, rising from 20 to 30 percent of the population. In fact, all age groups got heavier during the '80s. Only 15 percent of children were considered obese in the 1970s; by 1991, 21 percent of children fell into that category. Today, more than 58 million Americans are considered obese, and that number is growing.

Obesity is not an isolated disorder, but one that increases the risk of contracting other life-threatening illnesses, such as adult-onset diabetes, heart disease, high blood pressure, and common forms of cancer. People who are obese very often suffer from a host of other health problems.

What is so frustrating is that so many people became obsessed with achieving good health during the 1980s. You could hardly drive down the street without seeing not one jogger, but several—and all of them sweating profusely. Meanwhile, people limited their fat and cholesterol intake and included more carbohydrate-rich foods in their diets. Weight loss programs boomed during the '80s. Not only did many old and familiar programs thrive, but we also saw a profusion of new weight loss regimens that people adopted with alacrity. During any one year, more than 80 million Americans are on some kind of weight loss diet. Despite these sincere efforts, we are heavier and in many cases far sicker today than we were before the health craze took hold.

What are we doing wrong today and, more specifically, what happened in the 1980s?

The answer to that question begins with the recognition that we have forgotten the past—or, to be more specific, we forgot the way of life that we were designed to follow, the lifestyle that keeps us lean and promotes our health.

GOOD HEALTH, WEIGHT, AND THE HUMAN LIFESTYLE

The human body's design emerged slowly over millions of years of evolution, during which time our early ancestors slowly adapted to the earth's environment in order to survive and even thrive.

One of the most important aspects of nature to which we had to adapt was our food supply. The foods that were most abundant to early humans were plants, such as tubers, edible roots, fruits, and leafy vegetables. In addition to these, our ancestors also ate varying amounts of animal foods, which on the whole were leaner than those we get today in the supermarket. Thanks to a lot of old B-movies, many of us have a picture of our ancient ancestors as spear-toting tribespeople who took on giant mammoths and long-fanged beasts that resembled wild boar. In fact, for most of our existence, we didn't possess anything resembling a spear. Such tools didn't appear until perhaps 50,000 years ago, which meant that for nearly two million years, we had only the crudest of tools—mostly stones that were chipped along the edges and used as rudimentary hand axes. You can be sure that such tools, if they were ever used as weapons, did not make much of an impression on a herd of giant mammoths or irritated wildebeests.

The animals we did manage to kill were probably small game, which on the whole did not provide much food and certainly not many calories. On those rare opportunities when we got a chance to eat a larger animal, it was probably killed or wounded by some other means—either by another animal or by some form of accident. Although our ancient ancestors are known today as hunter-gatherers, a far more accurate way of describing them would be to call them scavenger-gatherers, because that's how they survived. They scavenged for food—both plant and animal foods.

The food supply for our Paleolithic forebears fluctuated wildly. It was marked by regular food shortages and sometimes lengthy famines. This made life precarious and in turn demanded that our ancestors conserve energy, or calories, whenever possible.

A fluctuating food supply encouraged people to rely heavily upon plant foods for their survival because they were easier to obtain than animal foods. Finding and digging up enough roots and tubers, or harvesting enough fruit or leafy vegetables, was hard work, to be sure, but that job was easier and more energy efficient than tracking a small animal through the forest, finally catching up to it, and then somehow managing to subdue it with a rock.

Scientists have confirmed this fact by studying the lives of traditional peoples who still follow a Paleolithic lifestyle, such as the !Kung of Botswana, who have been studied by Dr. A. S. Truswell of the Department of Nutrition and Food Science at the University of London. Truswell has found that it requires the !Kung women four hours to gather 1,000 calories of plant food; by contrast it takes the men 10 hours to return home with 1,000 calories of meat. Meat and fowl require more than twice the energy—and considerably more time—to harvest than plants. It's fairly safe to say that much of the time our ancient ancestors relied upon plant foods for the bulk of their nutrition and supplemented that, as much as they could, with animal foods.

Because plants were so abundant in the early human diet, our forebears evolved on highly nutritious and fiber-rich foods. It's been estimated that the traditional human diet had at least five to 10 times the fiber content of the modern diet. These unprocessed plant foods contained much less salt than our modern fare—one-tenth to one-fifth the quantity of salt we eat today—and provided higher levels of most vitamins and minerals than the diet we eat today.

Another big difference between our ancestral diet and today's regimen was that the meat our ancestors ate was relatively low in fat. In a study published in the *New England Journal of Medicine,* S. Boyd Eaton, M.D., and Melvin Konner, Ph.D., found that the average body fat of 15 species of wild animals living in Africa was only 3.9 percent. That amounts to about 20 to 25 percent total calories in fat. Common cuts of meat today derive anywhere from 30 to 80 percent of their total calories from fat.

The ancestral diet, therefore, offered high nutrient density, high fiber, and low fat.

A LOW-CALORIE DENSE DIET

It was also low in calorie density. A diet that is rich in whole, unprocessed plant foods and low in animal fats is generally a diet low in calorie density. Because they are so rich in fiber and water, vegetables and fruits are exceedingly low in calorie density. So, too, are minimally processed grains and beans. The chart below reveals just how low in calorie density such foods really are.

FOOD	CALORIES PER POUND (range)
NATURAL AND UNPROCESSED PLANT FOODS	
Vegetables	60 to 205
Fruits	140 to 420
Potatoes, yams, brown rice, whole-wheat pasta, and hot cereals	240 to 630
Beans, peas, lentils (cooked)	310 to 780
MEAT AND FISH	
Game meat, i.e., antelope, buffalo, rabbit, deer	600 to 860
Shellfish, i.e., shrimp, lobster, scallops	450 to 750
Lean fish, i.e., cod, halibut, haddock, flounder	400 to 600
Fatty fish, i.e., salmon, mackerel, trout, sea bass	660 to 900

KEY CHARACTERISTICS OF THE PREHISTORIC HUMAN DIET

The diet we evolved on, therefore, had the following characteristics:

1. The plant foods were whole and unprocessed, which made them exceedingly rich in nutrients and fiber.

2. The animal foods were low in fat.

3. The diet was low in salt.

4. The diet was low in calorie density.

This diet helped to shape our biological design and defined the kinds of foods we were best suited to consume.

HIGH ACTIVITY AND FREQUENT EATING

Not only was the diet relatively low in calorie density, but the lifestyle itself was extremely active. The simple act of obtaining food was physically demanding. Walking for miles to find food and then digging it up, climbing trees, or stalking a wild animal—all of this and more required tremendous effort and represented a tremendous energy expenditure. Of course, this says nothing about dealing with weather, rough terrain, avoiding dangerous animals, and coping with the elements. In short, our ancestors burned lots of calories just to stay alive.

In order to maintain adequate calorie levels, and therefore sustain their energy levels, our ancestors had to eat as many times as they could each day. Researchers have estimated that they ate anywhere from six to 12 times per day, which meant, in essence, that they ate every time they found food. That only stands to reason, however, since their last meal probably provided only enough calories to meet the demands of the next few hours or the remainder of the day. Our ancestors lived each day as if they were eating in Chinese restaurants. Frequent eating, therefore, was essential for survival.

ONE LONG, CONSISTENT PATTERN SUDDENLY INTERRUPTED

The diet we evolved on stayed pretty much the same right up to the time when agriculture developed, some 10,000 years ago. At that point, many cultures around the world became increasingly dependent for their existence on unprocessed, whole grains, vegetables, beans, and fruits. With the rise in agriculture and our increasing dependence upon plant foods, our meat consumption remained second to that of vegetables. Agriculture very likely brought about a drop in our consumption of animal foods. Even up through the 19th century, the foods people typically ate were largely unprocessed and whole, which meant that they were still rich in nutrient density and fiber. Our reliance upon plants is still evident in virtually every traditional culture that maintains our ancient ways of living. When we look at the diets of traditional people living in, say, Mexico, China, New Guinea, India, Africa, Brazil, and Panama, we see an abundance of plant foods and a smaller supply of animal foods. Depending on their climatic conditions, people rely upon everything from wheat, barley rice, corn, and millet to potatoes, yams, and a wide variety of vegetables and fruits as their staple foods. As for their animal food consumption, these traditional people eat smaller quantities of beef, fish, and poultry than modern cultures.

It's no coincidence that the people who still follow their traditional ways of eating tend to be lean and have very low rates of heart disease, adult-onset diabetes, many cancers, and obesity. Their differences cannot be due to genetics since migration studies clearly demonstrate that the same diseases of affluence that affect Westernized peoples also affect traditional people when they move to the West and adopt Westernized ways of eating and living.

Unfortunately, the ancient way of eating has been largely discarded for a diet that is very different from the one we evolved on. The primary differences, of course, are the dramatic increases in our consumption of fat and processed foods.

FROM WHOLE FOODS TO PROCESSED AND PARTIAL

Food processing is a very ancient art that dates back thousands of years. The first processed foods were probably sugars, breads, and bean products. Salting, pickling, and fermenting were common throughout Europe, the Middle East and Asia. (Archeologists and historians tell us that the daily drink served to the ancient Egyptians who built the pyramids was beer, which only adds to the mystery of how those magnificent structures ever got built.)

In most cases, the bread, pasta, tortillas, and other common grain products were still made with whole grains that were minimally processed. That meant that they were still rich in nutrients and fiber. These processed foods made up only a small percentage of the traditional human diet, however. In effect, our ancestors had no choice but to eat an abundance of whole, unprocessed foods.

All of that changed during the 20th century, when processed foods became vastly more common. Unlike our ancestors, however, modern food manufacturers took food processing many steps further. Not only did they dry and grind whole foods, but they also stripped the grain of its fiber and many important nutrients. The result is a food composed mostly of concentrated carbohydrates with lots of rapidly absorbed calories.

To add insult to injury, food manufacturers created processed foods that were passed off as "health foods" because they were low in fat. Throughout the 1970s and '80s, the primary health concern in the American diet was fat, and with good reason, since it was linked with high rates of heart disease, cancer, adult-onset diabetes, and obesity. As people became more aware of the dangers of fat and cholesterol, food manufacturers began turning out more and more processed foods that were low in fat or fat free. These foods were suddenly trumpeted as being good for your health. But just the opposite was true. By extracting the water and fiber—along with many important nutrients—food manufacturers had concentrated the foods' calories, making them high in calorie density and low in nutrients. Foods that people thought were good for their health—and especially good for their weight—were, in fact, causing dramatic increases in weight, which is one of the major reasons why so many people gained so much weight in the 1980s.

In a sense, food manufacturers had pulled off one of the great con games of the century: They hoodwinked people into thinking that "low-fat" or "fat-free" foods actually means "low in calories," and therefore good for weight loss. We, the American consumers, got all worked up over fat and cholesterol, never realizing that processed carbohydrates could be just about as bad—at least as far as weight loss is concerned.

By the early 1990s, supermarkets were flooded with foods that were high in carbohydrates and low in fat: cookies, cakes, chips, muffins, dried cereals, granola bars, and popcorn. Like proverbial wolves in sheep's clothing, a lot of these foods looked absolutely innocuous, but they were the secret causes of overweight.

Critics blamed America's burgeoning weight problem on high-carbohydrate diets, failing to realize that there is a very big difference between processed and unprocessed carbohydrate foods. Whole and unprocessed vegetables, whole grains, beans, and fruit are uniformly low in calorie density and ideal for both health and weight loss. But processed carbohydrate-rich foods are high-calorie bombs.

FOOD	CALORIES PER POUND (range)
UNPROCESSED FOODS WITH LITTLE OR NO FAT	
Dried fruit, jams, fake-fat potato chips, fat-free muffins, and breads, both whole grain and refined, including sourdough rolls, bagels, pita breads and baguettes	1,100 to 1,500
Dried cereal, pretzels, fat-free cookies, and fat-free potato chips	1,480 to 1,910
Raisins	1,360
Sugar, white	1,730
Sugar, brown	1,690

When fat is added to processed foods, the numbers begin to skyrocket. The following chart tells the story.

HIGH-FAT, PROCESSED FOODS	
French fries	1,400 to 1,500
Regular salad dressing	1,700 to 2,400
Cheese, sausages, bologna, bacon	1,270 to 2,300
Croissants	1,840
M & Ms	2,270
Oreo Cookies	2,200
Chocolate bars, doughnuts, pastries, granola bars	1,190 to 2,780
Potato chips, corn chips, Pringles, nuts, seeds	2,400 to 3,260
Butter and margarine	3,250
Olive oil, corn oil, lard, shortening	4,000 to 4,100

LOW CALORIE DENSITY, RICH IN NUTRIENTS

Interestingly, calorie density is not only associated with weight, but also with nutrient density and therefore with overall health. In general, foods that are low in calorie density are also high in nutrient content. Natural and unprocessed foods—vegetables, fruits, grains, and beans—are low in calorie density, but rich in nutrients. Processed foods and those rich in fat are usually high in calorie density, but low in nutrients. This may be another reason why people who eat low-calorie dense foods are both leaner and healthier than those who eat high-calorie dense foods. A diet composed mostly of low-calorie dense foods is associated with a reduced risk of cancer, heart disease, high blood pressure, adult-onset diabetes, and obesity. On the other hand, people who regularly eat high-calorie dense foods are not only more likely to be obese, but also run the risk of being undernourished.

It's true that you can create a low-calorie dense meal with foods that are low in nutrients and fiber—egg whites, chicken soup, white rice, pasta, and Jell-O are all low in calorie density—but in general, the foods with the lowest calorie density are also the ones with a high nutrient density.

Thus, as calorie density goes down, nutrient content tends to go up—and vice versa: As calorie density goes up, nutrient content tends to go down, often dramatically.

The chart below reveals the associated characteristics of foods that are either low or high in calorie density.

LOW-CALORIE DENSE FOODS TEND TO BE:	HIGH-CALORIE DENSE FOODS TEND TO BE:
Richer in nutrients	Lower in nutrient content
Minimally processed	More processed and refined
Lower in fat content	Higher in fat content

As I said in Chapter 1, foods that are low in calorie density also provide high satiety value, meaning they fill you up on the fewest calories. High satiety foods provide far less calories before you are full, or sated.

THEN AND NOW

The traditional human diet, based primarily on whole and unprocessed plant foods and low-fat animal fare, contained more nutrients, more fiber, and fewer calories, while the modern diet has more fat, more sugar, salt, processed carbohydrates, and an overall higher calorie density. We have deprived ourselves of adequate quantities of phytochemicals and the antioxidants—especially the carotenoids and vitamins C and E—that have been shown to reduce our risk of cancer and other diseases. It's as if we have turned the diet we've eaten for millions of years into a photographic negative of itself.

In addition to changes in the diet, we also became increasingly sedentary, which meant that we burned fewer calories than our bodies consumed. The result, of course, is weight gain.

Exercise provides a host of benefits that encourage weight reduction. First, exercise keeps insulin levels low, which means it promotes fat-burning. It also promotes muscle development. Increased muscle mass increases your ability to burn fat. Having more muscle is like having a car with more horsepower. A Corvette and a Toyota Corolla have very different capacities to burn fuel when you put the pedal to the metal, just as bigger muscles burn more fuel than smaller ones. But keep in mind they both burn the same amount when they're sitting in the garage. On the other hand, long periods on the couch will turn your Corvette body into a Corolla.

Here's a brief comparison between the traditional human diet and lifestyle versus the modern way of living.

TRADITIONAL HUMAN DIET	MODERN DIET
Richer in nutrients	Lower in nutrient content
Richer in plant foods	Low in plant foods
Low fat	High fat
Low salt	High salt
Whole, minimally processed	Highly refined and processed
High nutrient density	Low nutrient density
High fiber	Low fiber

TRADITIONAL HUMAN DIET	MODERN DIET
Low calorie concentration/density	High calorie concentration/density
High activity	Low activity

WHEN THE DIET CHANGED, SO DID OUR HEALTH

Scientists established long ago that the primary cause of coronary heart disease, many forms of cancer, obesity, and adult-onset diabetes is a diet rich in fat, cholesterol, processed foods, and calories. Two of those conditions—overweight and adult-onset diabetes—are caused directly by diets high in calorie density, little fiber, and lack of exercise. Not surprisingly, like obesity, the number of people with adult-onset diabetes is now skyrocketing in the United States and much of the developing world.

WHERE THE ANSWERS EXIST—AND DON'T EXIST

As I mentioned at the outset of this chapter, new weight-loss and health-promotion programs are being created almost daily. Meanwhile, scientists search for a genetic answer to obesity, adult-onset diabetes, and other degenerative diseases. The hunt for a genetic solution is particularly disingenuous because it leads people away from the real causes and cure for obesity and degenerative diseases—the calorie density of our foods, the dearth of important nutrients, and our lack of physical activity. It also causes people to believe that their genetic makeup defines their destiny. That is patently untrue. Genes can and do make us more susceptible to one illness or another. But in most cases we must create the environmental conditions needed for those genes to express themselves. People who have a genetic tendency for obesity or adult-onset diabetes do not necessarily have to contract those disorders.

A perfect illustration of this fact is the Pima Indians. Thousands of years ago, when their ancestors came to the Americas from Asia, the Pima Indians divided into two branches, one of which settled in what is now Arizona, while another branch took up residence in Mexico. For most of their existence, both tribes survived according to their traditional ways, producing a wide variety of plant foods on their land and subsisting on diets made up essentially of grains, vegetables, fruit, and small amounts of animal products. Early in this century, the U.S. government diverted the river that fed the lands of the Arizona Pimas, forcing them to give up their agricultural lifestyle and depriving them of their traditional diet. Unable to feed themselves, the Arizona Pimas were now obliged to accept government surplus foods, which transformed their diets from low-calorie dense fare to foods exceptionally high in calorie density. Their intake of lard, sugar, and refined flour increased dramatically.

The effect of such a diet on the Arizona Pimas was devastating. Today, the Arizona Pimas have the highest rates of adult-onset diabetes in the world and one of the highest rates of obesity. By the age of 50, more than 50 percent of the Arizona Pimas have adult-onset diabetes and most die prematurely. There is no doubt that they have a genetic susceptibility to both diabetes and obesity, but that susceptibility is expressed in response to their high-calorie dense diets, coupled with a sedentary lifestyle.

Interestingly, their relatives living in Mexico, who have remained on their traditional regimen, have enjoyed better health. Very few of the Mexican Pimas suffer from Type 2 diabetes, even though they have the same genetic potential for this disease as their Arizona cousins. Moreover, the Mexican Pimas average 60 to 65 pounds less body weight than the Arizona Pimas.

The Mexican Pimas, however, live on a diet made up of corn tortillas, beans, squash, rice, potatoes, pasta, vegetable soups, and a relatively narrow variety of vegetables. They do drink some soda pop and coffee and fry their beans in small amounts of vegetable oils, but rarely eat meat and poultry. In other words, their diet is low in fat and refined carbohydrates and rich in plant foods—a diet much lower in calorie density than their Arizona relatives. Consequently, their genetic susceptibility to obesity and diabetes is not expressed. On the contrary, they enjoy remarkably good health.

Both groups of Pimas possess the same genetic strengths and weaknesses. But only one group is healthy, because it adheres to a diet and lifestyle that supports the human design.

THERE IS A ROAD BACK

Illness—even severe disease—can be overcome. There is a way back to good health, healthy weight, and renewed vitality. The traditional human diet and lifestyle can create the conditions that restore the body's own healing forces—abilities that are incredibly powerful.

This was demonstrated by Dr. Terry T. Shintani, who, in 1990, used one form of the traditional diet to restore the health of a population of native Hawaiians who suffered from severe obesity and a wide variety of degenerative diseases.

Native Hawaiians, people of Asian descent who settled in Hawaii thousands of years ago, have the lowest life expectancy of any ethnic people in the United States, thanks largely to their exceedingly high rates of obesity, coronary heart disease, high blood pressure, and adult-onset diabetes. Dr. Shintani and his colleagues arranged to have 20 native Hawaiians adopt their traditional Hawaiian diet for only 21 days. The diet, which derived only seven percent of its total calories from fat, was made up largely of taro root, sweet potato, yams, breadfruit, greens, fruit, seaweed, fish, and chicken. While on the native regimen, the Hawaiians experienced a dramatic decrease in blood fats, or triglycerides, blood pressure, and weight. On average, they lost nearly 20 pounds in three weeks! They also reduced their risk of suffering a heart attack, contracting cancer, and adult-onset diabetes.

The transformation was startling to most observers, but we at the Pritikin Longevity Center have been using a similar program to accomplish even more remarkable turn-arounds in health. For example, our drop in serum cholesterol is over twice as great as that which Shintani's program effected. We bring about more dramatic results because we limit poultry and fish more than he did.

THE TRUE CURE

The Pritikin Program goes right to the heart of the problem, which is why it provides perhaps the most powerful medicine for these and other health problems. As I mentioned in Chapter 1, the Pritikin Program is based on five fundamental principles, which are:

- Eat whole, unprocessed plant foods, which are low in calorie density.

- Eat foods low in fat, especially saturated fat, transfatty acids, and cholesterol.

- Be more active.

- Eat frequently.

- Avoid salty foods and limit salt intake.

Like our ancestors, we at the Pritikin Center encourage you to eat frequently throughout the day. We urge you to eat three, low-calorie dense meals per day, along with two or three snacks—also low in calorie density—between meals. We realize that this runs counter to most of the advice given by weight-loss programs today, but there is a lot of good science to back up our point of view. First, eating frequently keeps you from being hungry, which is the main reason most people fail on diets and therefore cannot maintain weight loss. Having to suffer being hungry just to lose weight is not an effective weight loss strategy. It's too destructive to the quality of your life. Eventually, chronic hunger is going to defeat your discipline and then you'll be eating everything in sight. In order to lose weight—and keep it off—you've got to be able to eat frequently. The scientific research has shown that people who eat frequently not only lose weight, but keep it off. This behavior, as I said earlier, is consistent with the pattern we evolved on. Our ancestors ate as many as 12 times a day, scientists have shown, and most of those meals consisted entirely of plant foods.

Most modern Americans, on the other hand, eat three meals per day. Many skip breakfast, or simply have a cup of coffee, which means they only eat two daily meals. Rather than reducing calorie intake, this behavior actually encourages overeating and even gorging, especially on high-fat foods. The reason, very simply, is that hunger triggers our innate "famine response," which triggers an overwhelming desire for high-calorie, high-fat foods. Those who eat infrequently are often driven to eat bigger meals that are extremely rich in calories, especially from fat.

In order for frequent eating to result in significant weight loss, however, your meals and snacks must be low in calorie density. Essentially, we are encouraging you to utilize the "Chinese restaurant response" as a tool for good health and weight loss. As you know, Chinese food fills your stomach and creates satiety, but two hours later you're starving again. Why? Because many Chinese dishes are loaded with water and fiber, which make them low in calorie density and ideal for weight loss. In essence, they fill you up on very few calories, which is why, two hours later, you're hungry again. As long as you follow up that meal with a low-calorie dense meal or snack, you'll continue to keep your calories low, even though you're eating every few hours. By doing this, you'll be avoiding hunger as you lose weight.

That's what we want you to accomplish on the Pritikin Program: Satiety, or fullness, on a low-calorie density diet that is completely enjoyable and satisfying. This combination will give you good health and healthy weight.

9 | DISEASES OF MODERN LIFE

My father, Nathan Pritikin, was a successful inventor, engineer, and businessman. Though he never went to medical school, he had a passion for the study of health, medicine, and the health patterns of indigenous or traditional peoples. As far back as the 1940s, he began an assiduous study of medical literature, especially the science linking diet to degenerative diseases, such as heart disease, diabetes, cancer, and other illnesses. That study gave him insights into these illnesses that few people in the world had at the time, if anyone else had them at all.

In the 1950s, Nathan Pritikin was diagnosed with advanced coronary heart disease, the leading killer in the Western world. Armed with his knowledge of diet and its relationship to coronary heart disease, he developed a program of diet and exercise to treat and cure himself. Once he was well, he began to apply his approach to other sick people—at first informally, among people who came to him as a last resort, and then at the Pritikin Longevity Center, in Santa Barbara, California, which he officially opened on January 5, 1976.

At first he had only one doctor working with him and a few cooks, who were under the direction of my mother. As many readers know, the results my father experienced against these so-called "incurable" illnesses were nothing short of miraculous. People from all over the world flocked to Santa Barbara, and later to Santa Monica. Many had been told by their doctors that their diseases were "terminal," meaning there was no hope of recovery. Others were scheduled for coronary bypass surgery and told that if they did not have the surgery, they would soon be dead. Some arrived in wheelchairs, a few on stretchers. When they left our center, most were walking; many were running. The vast majority were restored to what my father used to term "normal function," meaning that they felt and behaved as if there was no presence of disease—as long as they remained on the Pritikin diet and exercise regimen. Because heart disease, high blood pressure, adult-onset diabetes, and so many other illnesses that we successfully treated were regarded as "incurable," we became known as the Lourdes of California. We were also the focal point of tremendous controversy, mostly for the same reasons.

We survived the controversy and even succeeded primarily because our results were medically and scientifically proven. Yes, they were astounding, but they were all based on solid science and all our recovery stories were medically documented. We had an array of outside researchers come into the center and study the effects of our program on the health of those who adopted it. We've been doing that ever since.

In fact, no diet and health program available to the public at large has been subjected to more rigorous scientific scrutiny than the Pritikin Program. And no program has demonstrated time and again its efficacy against the most dangerous degenerative diseases. We don't make a single claim that isn't supported by medical literature. When we say that our program has helped restore health to people with heart disease, adult-onset diabetes, high blood pressure, obesity, and other serious disorders, and that it has dramatically reduced people's risk factors for these same illnesses, as well as for cancer, we are stating a proven fact.

As I said in the Introduction, we have always offered a diet made up predominantly of low-calorie dense foods. In effect, the Pritikin Eating Plan always included the calorie density principles—at least in a somewhat less developed way. In the past we did allow more dried and concentrated calories, but because the availability of low-fat processed foods was much lower then, we didn't need a clearly defined calorie density principle in the same way we do today. Now, there are so many processed foods that are low in fat and high in calorie density that we really must have a calorie density solution in order to steer people correctly through the myriad pitfalls that await anyone who attempts to lose weight or regain their health using diet and exercise.

More than 70,000 people have come to the Pritikin Longevity Centers and all of them have been treated with the diet and exercise program I have described in this book. Allow me to summarize the causes of most degenerative diseases and our proven results in treating those illnesses with the Pritikin Program's Calorie Density Solution.

CORONARY HEART DISEASE: THE WORLD'S LEADING KILLER

Coronary heart disease is one of the most common forms of cardiovascular disease, a collection of illnesses that includes high blood pressure and stroke. Coronary heart disease arises when cholesterol plaques—also known as atherosclerosis—form within the arteries that bring blood to the heart muscle. As these plaques grow inside the heart's arteries, they reduce and can eventually cut off blood flow leading to the heart muscle. Without adequate blood flow, a part of the heart muscle can die, an event called a heart attack. The same process can occur in the arteries to the brain. When blood flow to the brain is blocked, a part of the brain can die, a condition referred to as a stroke. Both events can be lethal.

Long before a heart attack occurs, a person can suffer from periodic and severe chest pain, also called angina pectoris. Angina occurs when the heart is deprived of adequate oxygen.

The two primary dietary substances that cause the formation of atherosclerosis and thus form the basis for coronary heart disease are saturated fat, a form of fat found mostly in animal foods, and cholesterol, a sterol that exists only in animal foods. Plant foods have no cholesterol; most plant foods are free of saturated fat, as well.

Both saturated fat and cholesterol cause blood cholesterol levels to rise. The higher your blood cholesterol, the greater the likelihood that you will form cholesterol plaques in your arteries, including your coronary arteries and the arteries that lead to your brain.

With continued exposure to high blood cholesterol levels, the cholesterol plaques become increasingly volatile and unstable. Eventually, the plaque can rupture. Once that happens, an open wound forms within the inner wall of the artery. In an effort to close that wound, clotting substances in the blood form a blood clot that can be large enough to block blood flow, either to the heart or brain.

The critical factor in this process, of course, is your blood cholesterol level. Blood cholesterol, which is measured in milligrams per deciliter of blood (or mg/dl), is considered safe when it is at or below 150 mg/dl. Your risk of heart attack increases significantly when your cholesterol level exceeds 180 mg/dl. The average cholesterol level in the United States. is 210 mg/dl.

By substantially reducing the amount of saturated fat and cholesterol in your diet, the Pritikin Program dramatically reduces your blood cholesterol level. As blood cholesterol levels fall, the plaques inside your arteries are stabilized, meaning they are less likely to burst open and form clots inside your arteries. Indeed, when cholesterol levels fall to 150 mg/dl or lower, the liquid pools of cholesterol inside the plaque begin to drain, causing the plaques to shrink. As they get smaller, more blood and oxygen are allowed to flow to the heart, brain, and other organs. Angina pain tends to decrease— and in many cases is eliminated entirely—when this occurs, as well.

A diet made up primarily of whole grains, vegetables, beans, fruit, and smaller amounts of low-fat animal products is the key to lower cholesterol levels and stabilization and shrinkage of atherosclerotic plaques. In fact, the process of stabilizing and shrinking the plaques occurs within days of beginning the Pritikin Program. In time, such a diet can reverse the cholesterol plaques, studies have shown.

In addition to fat and cholesterol, another key dietary constituent is fiber, which has been shown to independently lower cholesterol. The Pritikin Eating Plan, as I have been saying, is especially rich in fiber.

Finally, it's also important to get regular exercise in order to strengthen your heart and other muscles.

THE PRITIKIN RESULTS AGAINST CORONARY HEART DISEASE

DRAMATIC DECLINES IN CHOLESTEROL LEVELS

Numerous studies have evaluated the effects of the Pritikin Program on participants at the Pritikin Center at Santa Monica. Researchers showed that after three weeks on the Pritikin Program, a population of 4,597 people experienced a 23 percent drop in cholesterol and a 33 percent drop in blood fats, or triglycerides. Research has shown that a 1 percent drop in cholesterol indicates a 2 percent drop in the risk of heart attack, which meant that the 23 percent drop in cholesterol created by the Pritikin Program provided a 46 percent drop in the risk of these potential lethal events. The findings showing this remarkable drop in blood cholesterol were published in the *Archives of Internal Medicine* (151:1389. 1991) and *The New England Journal of Medicine* (323:1921. 1990).

INCREASED BLOOD FLOW TO THE HEART

In another study, UCLA researchers used advanced nuclear technology known as PET Scanning to demonstrate that 13 participants experienced significant improvement of blood flow through the coronary arteries to the heart muscle after just six weeks on the Pritikin Program. This study demonstrated the power of the program to improve the condition of the coronary arteries—and thus take patients out of immediate danger of having a heart attack—within a relatively short period of time. *Circulation* (92:197-204. 1995).

AVOIDING BYPASS SURGERY AND RELIEVING CHEST PAIN

Other research has shown that the Pritikin Program can be an effective alternative to bypass surgery as well as an antidote to angina pectoris, or chest pain. Researchers studied 64 people who were scheduled for coronary bypass surgery but chose to adopt the Pritikin Program instead. Five years later, researchers found that 81 percent of these people still had not had bypass surgery.

Of those who came to the Longevity Center taking medication for angina, 62 percent left the center free of all medication for chest pain. Many of the remaining people had reduced their medication substantially. The findings, as well as those regarding the bypass surgery, were published in the *Journal of Cardiac Rehabilitation* (3:183. 1983).

HIGH BLOOD PRESSURE: THE SILENT KILLER

High blood pressure, or hypertension, affects more than 60 million Americans and is the most common cardiovascular disease today. People with hypertension are seven times more likely to have a stroke as those who do not have high blood pressure; they have five times the risk of congestive heart failure and four times the risk of heart attack.

Like coronary heart disease, high blood pressure is far more common in the Western industrialized world than in Third World nations, such as countries in Africa and New Guinea. Unlike its other Asian neighbors, Japan has a high incidence of hypertension, as well, primarily because they—like so many of us in the United States—consume high levels of salt.

Salt is one of the primary causes of high blood pressure. Other causes include a deficiency of plant nutrients in the diet, a lack of exercise, and obesity. Salt causes blood volume, also known as plasma, to increase. The result is an increase in pressure within the vascular system. Eventually, blood vessels can expand like a balloon and pop open. When such an event occurs in the brain, it is called a stroke.

The best treatment for hypertension includes the restriction of salt intake, weight loss, and an increase in vegetables, fruit, and exercise.

THE PRITIKIN PROGRAM AND HIGH BLOOD PRESSURE

After studying a group of 268 Pritikin participants at the Santa Monica Pritikin Longevity Center who were taking medication for proven hypertension, researchers found that 83 percent were able to achieve normal blood pressures and eliminate all hypertensive medication after just four weeks on the Pritikin Program.

Our program becomes all the more appealing for people with hypertension when you consider that the disorder is a potential killer and that the medication dramatically diminishes the quality of life for many who suffer from the condition.

DIABETES: A DANGEROUS DISEASE WITH A LOT OF TERRIBLE SIDE EFFECTS

There are two types of diabetes. Type 1, sometimes referred to as juvenile diabetes because it often arises in young people, especially children, occurs when people are unable to produce sufficient amounts of insulin to meet the body's needs. Insulin, you will recall, is a hormone that makes blood sugar available to cells. Type 2, often referred to as adult-onset diabetes, usually occurs in people older than 30. Many people with adult-onset diabetes produce more insulin than non-diabetics. Unfortunately, the body's cells are resistant to that insulin and thus prevent blood sugar from entering.

When cells become insulin-resistant, blood sugar and insulin rise to dangerous levels within the blood, causing a host of dangerous side effects. People with diabetes are two to four times more likely than healthy people to suffer a heart attack and two to three times more likely to suffer a stroke. Diabetics are far more likely to contract intermittent claudication (reduced blood flow within the legs, often causing severe pain), tingling and burning feelings in the fingers and toes, gangrene, amputation, retinopathy, blindness, and kidney failure.

Approximately 15 million Americans have some form of diabetes. More than 90 percent of them suffer from adult-onset diabetes. There is no cure for Type 1 diabetes, but many with Type 2 diabetes can reverse their disorder and live medication-free. It's important for people with either type of diabetes to adopt the Pritikin Program, however, because our diet and exercise approach reduces the risk of diabetic side effects, including heart disease and kidney failure.

The primary causes of adult-onset diabetes are obesity and a lack of exercise. These two factors combine to make muscle cells resistant to insulin, research has shown. The most effective ways of preventing and reversing adult-onset, or Type 2, diabetes, are to adopt the Pritikin Program and lose weight.

Overweight and obesity, as I have shown in this book, are caused primarily by a diet made up predominantly of foods high in calorie density, along with a lack of physical exercise.

THE PRITIKIN PROGRAM AND ADULT-ONSET DIABETES

As I said, it's important for people with either Type 1 or Type 2 diabetes to adopt the Pritikin Program because it can prevent many of the major side effects of the illness. For those with Type 2 diabetes, however, we can do a lot toward mitigating the disorder or help to overcome it entirely. Researchers studied the effects of the Pritikin diet on 652 adult-onset diabetics, many of whom were taking either insulin or oral medication when they arrived at the Pritikin Longevity Center. The scientists found that of those who were taking insulin, 39 percent left the center insulin-free. Of those who were taking diabetic oral medication when they adopted the Pritikin Program, 70 percent left the center off all oral medication, having achieved normal blood sugar levels. These results were published in *Diabetes Care* (17:1469. 1994).

As our results have consistently shown, the Pritikin Program is perhaps the most effective non-pharmacological treatment available for adult-onset diabetes anywhere.

CANCER: STAY AWAY FROM THE POISONS

Virtually all the research on the relationship between diet and cancer have shown that populations that eat a diet low in fat and high in plant nutrients, including fiber, have a lower incidence of the common cancers, especially those of the breast, colon, and prostate. Conversely, science has consistently shown that a diet rich in fat and low in fiber and plant nutrients is associated with a higher incidence of the common cancers.

Excess consumption of saturated fat, commonly found in animal foods, is associated with a higher incidence of prostate cancer. Polyunsaturated fats, found mostly in vegetable oils, appear to promote the growth of some cancers when consumed in excess. When it comes to breast cancer, many diet and lifestyle factors may combine either to promote the onset of the illness, or prevent it. Women who exercise and eat a diet low in fat and high in fiber and plant nutrients appear to have a lower incidence of breast cancer. Even lung cancer may well have a dietary component. Though clearly related to cigarette smoking, lung cancer incidence is higher among those who smoke cigarettes and eat a high-fat diet than those who smoke cigarettes and eat a low-fat, high-plant diet.

Science is now showing that people whose diets are rich in whole grains, fresh vegetables, beans, and fruits have a much lower risk of developing many types of cancer. These foods may strengthen the body's ability to destroy cancer cells, as well.

In addition to diet, exercise seems to provide some protection against many cancers.

THE PRITIKIN PROGRAM AND CANCER

Many types of cancers seem to need the right underlying conditions before they can be triggered and then take hold within the body Those underlying conditions are called risk factors. These risk factors not only help trigger the disease, but also promote its growth. Four separate studies looked at the effects of the Pritikin Program on certain risk factors for colon, prostate, and breast cancers and found that these risk factors were reduced by as much as 50 percent after people adopted the Pritikin Program. These studies were published in *Preventive Medicine* (17: 432. 1988); *Nutrition* (7:137. 1991); *Journal of the National Cancer Institute* (86: 146. 1994); *Cancer* (76:2491. 1995); *Nutrition and Cancer* (31:127, 1998).

WHY DOES IT WORK?

It's very possible that given the right conditions, and recognized early enough, the body is capable of healing itself of most diseases. You might say that the Pritikin Program's Calorie Density Solution provides the "right conditions." Those right conditions might be defined as follows:

1. The Program reduces cholesterol and all forms of fat, especially saturated fat, which, when consumed in excess, are highly toxic to the body. When the Program is followed optimally, it reduces these potential sources of disease to levels that the body can handle safely.

2. The Program reduces overall calorie intake by providing foods low in calorie density and high in satiety value. In this way, it helps you reduce your weight and keep it at a healthy level without having to count calories or endure chronic hunger in order to sustain weight loss.

3. It dramatically increases the levels of plant nutrients and fiber that you consume. These strengthen your immune system and your body's cancer-fighting forces. The fiber lowers calorie density, helps reduce your cholesterol level, and promotes the elimination of waste products from your body, as well.

4. Once on the Program, you're going to become more physically active. Increased physical activity causes you to burn more calories. It also enhances insulin sensitivity, causing you to burn more fat. Exercise strengthens your muscles, including your heart, and promotes blood and lymph circulation. It also strengthens your immune system.

Your body is a miraculous machine with awesome healing powers. All it needs is the right diet and daily activity to restore its health—in short, the Pritikin Program.

¹⁰ RECIPES

Here are 52 delicious recipes for foods for all occasions. No matter whether they are for breakfast, lunch, dinner, or dessert, these recipes offer dishes that are low in calorie density and high in nutrients. They will promote weight loss, if you are currently overweight, and good health.

There are a few things to keep in mind when you read these recipes. We use the term "lite" to describe soy sauces that are relatively lower in salt than standard soy sauce. The truth is, however, that all soy sauces are relatively high in salt—in fact, too high to be accurately referred to as "low-salt" on the label. Still, some soy sauces are indeed lower in salt than others. The natural foods industry has chosen to label these lower-salt soy sauces as "lite" soy sauce, a term we have adopted throughout the recipes for the sake of consistency, utility, and honesty.

We do use brand-name products in many of our recipes. We do this for two reasons. The first is that we know these foods meet the Pritikin standards for quality ingredients, as well as for fat and/or cholesterol content. The second is simply practicality: It's easier for you, the reader, to find these products on your grocer's shelves if we use the brand name.

Finally, our recipes meet a very high standard for the amount of fat, cholesterol, and salt they contain, as well as for their nutrient density and flavor. We pride ourselves on making foods that are health-promoting, weight-reducing, and delicious. As you will see by reading the recipes, the fat content of our dishes is extremely low—so low, in fact, that it's essentially irrelevant to list whether the fat is made up of monounsaturated, polyunsaturated, and saturated fats. Rest assured that the saturated fat content of these foods is extremely low and therefore extremely healthful. You do not have to worry about Pritikin foods containing anything but healthful amounts of fat.

Well, enough said. It's time now to dive into the recipes and enjoy your food—along with the good health and weight loss that will follow.

LIST OF RECIPES

LIST OF RECIPES *continued*

BROCCOMOLE

MAKES 16 ¼-CUP SERVINGS

½ cup canned, diced Ortega green chili peppers
1 tsp. minced garlic
1 cup chopped onions
4 cups overcooked broccoli florets
    (about 5 cups fresh)
2 tsp. lite soy sauce
pinch of grated nutmeg
1½ cups nonfat sour cream

NUTRITION INFORMATION

Each serving contains approximately:
40 calories
2 g protein
7 g carbohydrate
0 g total fat
0 mg cholesterol
62 mg sodium
1.4 g dietary fiber
4% calories from fat

Caloric Density: 231

Put peppers, garlic, and onions into a food processor fitted with the steel chopping blade and pulse until finely chopped. Add the broccoli and pulse until it is also chopped finely. Add the soy sauce, nutmeg, and sour cream and process until the mixture is creamy.

Chill until ready to serve. Serve as a dip with a variety of sliced fresh vegetables.

HUMMUS

MAKES 6 ¼-CUP SERVINGS

3 medium cloves garlic
1 15-ounce can salt-free garbanzo beans, drained
2 Tbs. fresh lemon juice
1 Tbs. white wine Worcestershire sauce
1 tsp. Dijon mustard
1 tsp. natural rice vinegar
¼ tsp. sesame oil
chopped parsley or cilantro

NUTRITION
INFORMATION

Each serving contains
approximately:
67 calories
3 g protein
11 g carbohydrate
1.2 g total fat
0 mg cholesterol
35 mg sodium
2.7 g dietary fiber
16% calories from fat

Caloric Density: 652

In an empty food processor, fitted with the steel chopping blade, feed the garlic through the feed tube while the processor is running to chop the garlic.

Remove the lid and add the rest of the ingredients. Process until smooth.

Transfer the mixture to a bowl and chill until ready to serve. Garnish with chopped parsley or cilantro.

Serve as a spread or dip with raw vegetables, or use as a sandwich spread on whole-wheat bread or pita with sliced tomato, red onion, cucumber, and lettuce.

SALMON MOUSSE

MAKES 16 ¼-CUP SERVINGS

2 8-ounce cans reduced-sodium salmon, drained
1½ cups nonfat sour cream
1 cup cooked frozen artichoke hearts
    (or 1 cup salt-free, canned)
½ cup chopped green onions
1 Tbs. chopped fresh dill
2 tsp. Dijon mustard
1 Tbs. fresh lemon juice
1 Tbs. rinsed capers

NUTRITION INFORMATION

Each serving contains approximately:
76 calories
6 g protein
5 g carbohydrate
2.9 g total fat
7 mg cholesterol
72 mg sodium
0.6 g dietary fiber
35% calories from fat

Caloric Density: 492

Using the pulse setting, process the all ingredients in a food processor until smooth.

Refrigerate until chilled, about 1 hour before serving.

Serve as an appetizer with fresh vegetables or whole-grain crackers.

BALSAMIC ORANGE VINAIGRETTE

MAKES 10 2-TBS. SERVINGS

2 Tbs. water
1 cup fresh orange juice
2 tsp. corn starch
2 Tbs. balsamic vinegar
$^{1}/_{2}$ tsp. garlic powder
$^{1}/_{2}$ tsp. dried tarragon

NUTRITION
INFORMATION

Each serving contains
approximately:
18 calories
less than 1 g protein
4 g carbohydrate
0 g total fat
0 mg cholesterol
1 mg sodium
0 g dietary fiber
3% calories from fat

Caloric Density: 262

Place all the ingredients in a nonreactive saucepan and bring to a boil, stirring frequently. Allow the mixture to turn clear and thicken. Remove from heat. Use this dressing warm or at room temperature. Use as a marinade for fish and chicken, a coleslaw dressing, a dip for fresh vegetables, or as a salad dressing.

This will keep for up to seven days if refrigerated in a sealed jar.

CREAMY TOFU DRESSING

MAKES 6 $\frac{1}{4}$-CUP SERVINGS

$\frac{1}{2}$ tsp. mustard seeds
1 12.3-ounce package light "silken" tofu
$\frac{1}{4}$ cup 1% buttermilk
3 Tbs. natural rice vinegar
2 Tbs. Fruit Source syrup (or rice syrup)*
2 Tbs. white wine Worcestershire sauce
3 cloves garlic, minced
$\frac{1}{8}$ tsp. ground black pepper
1 Tbs. chopped green onion tops or chives

NUTRITION
INFORMATION

Each serving contains
approximately:
68 calories
4 g protein
10 g carbohydrate
less than 1 g total fat
0.3 mg cholesterol
116 mg sodium
minimal dietary fiber
12% calories from fat

Caloric Density: 334

Toast the mustard seeds in a small, dry skillet (not nonstick) over low heat just until they begin to pop (1 to 2 minutes). Let cool, then grind with a mortar and pestle, or crush them with the bottom of a heavy bottle. Blend the tofu, buttermilk, vinegar, Fruit Source syrup, white wine Worcestershire sauce, garlic, ground mustard seeds and black pepper in a food processor or blender until smooth. Stir in the green onion. Chill until ready to use (makes about 1$\frac{1}{2}$ cups dressing). Will keep for up to one week in the refrigerator.

Use as a creamy dressing for green salads or coleslaw, as a dip for raw vegetables, and as a topping for baked potatoes.

If 1% buttermilk can't be found, 2% can be used. This will raise the calories to 70, fat grams to 1 g per serving, and increase the caloric density to 342.

*Fruit Source is a fruit and grain based syrup usually found in health food stores.

THOUSAND ISLAND DRESSING

MAKES 1½ CUPS (2-TBS. SERVINGS)

1 cup nonfat yogurt
½ cup no-salt-added ketchup
1 Tbs. natural rice vinegar
1 tsp. lite soy sauce
½ tsp. Tabasco sauce
½ tsp. apple juice concentrate
1 tsp. vanilla extract
1 tsp. garlic powder
1 Tbs. no-salt-added Dijon mustard
1 Tbs. finely chopped celery
¼ tsp. prepared horseradish

NUTRITION INFORMATION

Each serving contains approximately:
26 calories
1 g protein
4 g carbohydrate
less than 1 g total fat
0 mg cholesterol
45 mg sodium
0 g dietary fiber
7% calories from fat

Caloric Density: 334

Served with ½ cup raw vegetables:

Caloric Density: 184

In a medium bowl, whisk together all the ingredients until smooth and creamy. Refrigerate in a nonaluminum (nonreactive) container. The dressing may have to be restirred to recombine the ingredients before use. It will keep for several days if kept refrigerated.

Use as a salad dressing, a dip for raw vegetables, or to make shrimp or Crab Louie.

BOWTIE PASTA CHICKEN SALAD

MAKES 4 2-CUP SERVINGS

8 ounces dry bowtie pasta
$\frac{1}{2}$ cup sliced green onion
1 ripe tomato, diced
vegetable oil cooking spray
$\frac{1}{2}$ pound boneless skinless chicken breast,
    cut into small chunks
$\frac{1}{2}$ cup nonfat, low-sodium chicken broth
2 tsp. cornstarch
2 Tbs. balsamic vinegar
1 tsp. Italian seasoning mix
1 cup broccoli florets
1 cup sliced green or red bell peppers
2 Tbs. fat-free Parmesan cheese

NUTRITION
INFORMATION

Each serving contains
approximately:
225 calories
22 g protein
24 g carbohydrate
3.5 g total fat
60 mg cholesterol
142 mg sodium
3.5 g dietary fiber
13% calories from fat

Caloric Density: 396

Cook bowtie pasta according to package directions. Drain in a colander and rinse with cold water to prevent further cooking. Place in a large mixing bowl along with the sliced green onion and diced tomatoes.

Lightly spray a nonstick skillet with vegetable oil cooking spray and heat over medium-high heat. Sauté the chicken until golden, about 3 minutes. Combine the chicken broth and the cornstarch and add to the skillet along with the balsamic vinegar and Italian seasoning mix. Bring to a boil, stirring constantly. Cook until the chicken chunks are almost done, about 4 minutes. Add the broccoli and peppers and cook for 4 minutes. Add the cooked chicken mixture to the bowl with the pasta along with the Parmesan cheese and toss well. Serve warm or chilled. Optional presentation: Serve the salad over shredded dark green lettuce.

BROCCOLI WALDORF SALAD

MAKES 4 1-CUP SERVINGS

2 cups sliced broccoli florets
2 red apples, cored and sliced (leave skin on)
1 cup light, fat-free vanilla flavored yogurt*
¼ cup sliced green onion
1 Tbs. chopped walnuts
¼ tsp. ground cinnamon

NUTRITION
INFORMATION

Each serving contains
approximately:
153 calories
8 g protein
30 g carbohydrate
less than 1 g total fat
0 mg cholesterol
79 mg sodium
11 g dietary fiber
5% calories from fat

Caloric Density: 252

Toss all the ingredients together well in a medium bowl. Refrigerate until ready to serve. This salad goes well with almost any entrée.

*Light yogurt is sweetened with aspartame instead of sugar and contains only about half the calories.

COLESLAW WITH CREAMY TOFU DRESSING

MAKES 6 1-CUP SERVINGS

3 cups shredded green or white cabbage
2 cups shredded red cabbage
1/2 yellow bell pepper, cut into strips
1/2 green bell pepper, cut into strips
1 1/2 cups Creamy Tofu Dressing (see page 160)
2 Tbs. chopped cilantro or parsley (optional)

NUTRITION
INFORMATION

Each serving contains
approximately:
92 calories
5 g protein
15 g carbohydrate
1 g total fat
0 mg cholesterol
126 mg sodium
2.2 g dietary fiber
10% calories from fat

Caloric Density: 230

In a large bowl, combine the shredded cabbages and yellow and green pepper strips. Add the Creamy Tofu Dressing and combine well. Stir in the cilantro or parsley, if using, and serve chilled.

LENTIL SALAD

MAKES 4 1-CUP SERVINGS

½ cup raw lentils
1½ cups water
½ cup chopped red onion
1 cup chopped red bell pepper
½ cup chopped green bell pepper
1 large tomato, chopped
2 Tbs. rice vinegar
1 Tbs. fresh lemon juice
1½ tsp. lite soy sauce
1½ tsp. Worcestershire sauce
1 tsp. no-salt-added Dijon mustard
½ tsp. minced garlic
2 scallions, sliced, including green tops
½ tsp. each dried oregano, tarragon,
    and dill (or 1 tsp. each fresh)

NUTRITION
INFORMATION

Each serving contains
approximately:
150 calories
8 g protein
28 g carbohydrate
less than 1 g total fat
0 mg cholesterol
123 mg sodium
10 g dietary fiber
4% calories from fat

Caloric Density: 232

In a medium saucepan over medium heat, cook the lentils, covered, in the 1½ cups water for 40 to 45 minutes, or until just tender. Drain well and refrigerate to cool.

In a large bowl combine the cooled lentils, onion, bell peppers, and chopped tomato. In a small bowl whisk together the vinegar, lemon juice, soy sauce, Worcestershire sauce, and mustard. Stir in the garlic. Pour the sauce into the lentil mixture and toss to mix. Add the scallions and herbs and toss again.

Serve either chilled or at room temperature as a salad.

Note: This dish may also be used as a room temperature side dish with grilled chicken or pork tenderloin.

It may also be used as a vegetarian main dish by adding 6 oz. cubed firm tofu (combine the tofu cubes with the dressing and mix gently with the lentil mixture).

ORANGE-BRAISED CHICKEN WITH
WATERCRESS AND FENNEL SALAD

MAKES 4 SERVINGS

vegetable oil cooking spray
2 chicken breast halves, skin and fat removed
$\frac{1}{2}$ tsp. salt-free lemon-pepper seasoning
1½ cups orange juice
peel of 1 orange, removed with a zester
   (or use a peeler and shred the peel with a knife)
1½ Tbs. balsamic vinegar
1½ Tbs. white wine Worcestershire sauce
1 cup chopped red onion
1 large fennel bulb, trimmed and sliced thin crosswise
1 Tbs. chopped fresh tarragon
1 bunch fresh watercress, trimmed and washed

NUTRITION
INFORMATION

Each serving contains
approximately:
174 calories
16 g protein
23 g carbohydrate
1.9 g total fat
36 mg cholesterol
148 mg sodium
4 g dietary fiber
10% calories from fat

Caloric Density: 260

Place a medium nonstick skillet over medium-high heat. Spray with vegetable oil cooking spray. Add the chicken breasts and sprinkle them with the lemon-pepper seasoning. Brown the chicken breasts lightly on both sides.

Remove the pan from the heat and allow it to cool a little. Lower the heat to medium-low, add the orange juice to the pan and simmer the chicken breasts, covered, turning occasionally, for about 10 minutes or until they are cooked through. Transfer the chicken to a cutting board and allow it to cool.

If necessary, simmer the orange juice remaining in the pan, uncovered, until it is reduced to about ⅔ cup. Add the orange peel, balsamic vinegar, white wine Worcestershire sauce and red onion and mix well.

In a large bowl, combine the sliced fennel with the orange-onion mixture. Add the tarragon and toss until well mixed. Slice the cooked chicken. On a large platter, make a bed of watercress. Using a slotted spoon, lift the fennel mixture from the bowl and mound it over the watercress, leaving some sauce in the bottom of the bowl. Arrange the sliced chicken over the fennel and drizzle the remaining sauce over it. Serve cold or at room temperature.

STIR-FRY TOFU SALAD

MAKES 4 2-CUP SERVINGS

NUTRITION
INFORMATION

4 cups shredded cabbage
8 ounces firm tofu, cut into cubes
$^1/_2$ cup orange juice
2 Tbs. lite soy sauce
2 Tbs. rice wine vinegar
$^1/_2$ Tbs. cornstarch
vegetable oil cooking spray
2 Tbs. minced garlic
1 Tbs. grated fresh ginger
1 cup sliced mushrooms
$^1/_2$ cup sliced celery
1 cup sliced carrots
2 cups mung bean sprouts
2 cups sliced broccoli

Each serving contains
approximately:
166 calories
11 g protein
27 g carbohydrate
4 g total fat
0 mg cholesterol
198 mg sodium
6 g dietary fiber
21% calories from fat

Caloric Density: 190

Place the shredded cabbage in a large mixing bowl and set it to the side. Place the tofu in a medium mixing bowl with the orange juice, soy sauce, vinegar and cornstarch. Allow to marinate while you prepare the rest of the ingredients.

Generously spray a large nonstick skillet with vegetable oil cooking spray and heat over medium-high heat. Sauté the garlic and ginger until light brown, about 1 minute. Add the mushrooms, celery, carrots, bean sprouts, and broccoli. Cook for 2 minutes, stirring frequently. Add the marinade from the tofu and bring to a boil, stirring well. Add the tofu and cook for 2 minutes.

Toss the warm stir-fry mixture with the cabbage and serve warm or chilled.

WARM SPINACH AND BEAN SALAD

MAKES 4 1½-CUP SERVINGS

5 cups fresh spinach leaves, washed and
    ready to serve (about 1 5-ounce bag)
olive oil cooking spray
1 cup chopped onions
2 tsp. minced garlic
1½ cups cooked pinto beans, drained
1 15-ounce can no-salt-added diced tomatoes
1 cup diced zucchini
3 Tbs. balsamic vinegar
¼ tsp. hot pepper sauce

NUTRITION
INFORMATION

Each serving contains
approximately:
153 calories
8 g protein
30 g carbohydrate
less than 1 g total fat
0 mg cholesterol
79 mg sodium
11 g dietary fiber
5% calories from fat

Caloric Density: 252

Place spinach leaves in a large salad bowl and very lightly mist with olive oil
cooking spray.

    Generously spray a large nonstick skillet with olive oil cooking spray and
heat over medium-high heat. Add the onions and garlic and sauté until golden,
about 1 minute. Add the beans, tomatoes, zucchini, vinegar, and hot pepper
sauce. Bring to a boil then reduce to a simmer. Cook until the zucchini is tender and most of the liquid has evaporated, about 8 to 10 minutes. Mash beans
lightly while cooking and stirring.

    Pour bean sauce over spinach leaves and toss together. Serve warm.

BLACK BEAN AND VEGETABLE STEW

MAKES 10 1½-CUP SERVINGS

1½ medium red onions, chopped
2 cloves garlic, minced
1 bay leaf
⅓ cup nonfat, low-sodium
    chicken or vegetable broth
1 medium carrot, diced
1 medium red bell pepper, diced
1 medium green bell pepper, diced
2 stalks celery, sliced
1 small jalapeño pepper,
    seeded and finely chopped
1 16-ounce can no-salt-added diced tomatoes
3 15-ounce cans no-salt-added black beans
    (including liquid)*
¾ cup red wine
½ tsp. dried thyme
1 tsp. dried oregano
1 Tbs. Worcestershire sauce
2 Tbs. lite soy sauce
2 Tbs. red wine vinegar
nonfat sour cream or yogurt (optional)

NUTRITION
INFORMATION

Each serving contains
approximately:
217 calories
12 g protein
38 g carbohydrate
less than 1 g total fat
0 mg cholesterol
176 mg sodium
12.8 g dietary fiber
4% calories from fat

Caloric Density: 205

In a large, heavy bottom Dutch oven or soup pot, sauté the onions, garlic, and bay leaf in the chicken or vegetable broth for 2 to 3 minutes. Add the carrots, bell peppers, celery, and jalapeño pepper and cook over medium heat, covered, stirring occasionally, for 5 minutes, then add the tomatoes and cook for 1 minute more. Add the canned beans (including the liquid), the red wine, herbs, Worcestershire and soy sauces, and vinegar. Cover the pot and cook over medium-low heat, stirring occasionally, until the vegetables are tender and the flavors well blended. Add a little extra broth if it becomes too dry. Remove the bay leaf and discard. Serve hot in shallow bowls, garnished with a dollop of nonfat sour cream or yogurt, if desired.

*If salt-free canned beans can't be found, rinse regular canned beans well and use ½ cup low-sodium vegetable or chicken broth instead of the liquid in the can. You can also substitute your own salt-free cooked dried beans and their cooking liquid.

CHICKEN CORN CHOWDER

MAKES 6 1-CUP SERVINGS

vegetable oil cooking spray
$^1/_2$ cup chopped onion
1 cup diced green pepper
1 pound skinless boneless
    chicken breast, cut into chunks
1$^1/_2$ cups nonfat, low-sodium chicken broth
3 Tbs. cornstarch
2 cups skim milk
1 potato, peeled and diced
1$^1/_2$ cups frozen corn kernels
1 bay leaf
$^1/_2$ tsp. dried thyme leaves
ground black pepper, to taste
1 Tbs. white wine Worcestershire sauce

NUTRITION INFORMATION

Each serving contains approximately:
200 calories
24 g protein
23 g carbohydrate
1.5 g total fat
45 mg cholesterol
172 mg sodium
2 g dietary fiber
7% calories from fat

Caloric Density: 282

Spray a 4- to 6-quart Dutch oven generously with vegetable oil cooking spray and heat over medium-high heat. Sauté the chopped onion and green pepper until golden brown, about 3 minutes. Add the chicken breast chunks and sauté briefly.

Combine the chicken broth with the cornstarch in a small mixing bowl and add to the Dutch oven along with the remaining ingredients. Bring the chowder to a boil, reduce the heat to low and simmer until the diced potato pieces are tender, about 10 minutes. Stir occasionally to keep the chowder from scorching. Remove the bay leaf.

Serve hot along with a generous tossed salad.

EASY CHICKEN SKILLET CHILI

MAKES 4 1½-CUP SERVINGS

1 tsp. ground cumin
1 tsp. chili powder
vegetable oil cooking spray
1 Tbs. minced garlic
1 cup diced onions
1 cup diced green peppers
1 chopped jalapeño pepper,
    stem, veins, and seeds removed
¾ pound skinless boneless chicken, cut into chunks
1 cup cooked pinto beans, drained
1 tsp. dried oregano leaves
2 cups chopped stewed no-salt-added tomatoes
1 Tbs. tomato paste
1 Tbs. natural rice vinegar
¼ cup water
chopped tomatoes (optional)
chopped green onions (optional)
nonfat sour cream (optional)

NUTRITION INFORMATION

Each serving contains approximately:
232 calories
25 g protein
26 g carbohydrate
3 g total fat
49 mg cholesterol
100 mg sodium
7.5 g dietary fiber
12% calories from fat

Caloric Density: 205

Heat a large nonstick skillet over medium-high heat. Place the cumin and chili powder in the pan and briefly swirl them around so they are toasted, about 30 seconds. Do not allow them to burn. Place them in a small bowl and set it aside. Allow the pan to cool.

Spray the pan with vegetable oil cooking spray and place back on the stove. Sauté the garlic, onions, and peppers until golden, about 3 minutes. Add the chicken and sauté for another 3 minutes. Add the rest of the ingredients, including the toasted spices and stir together. Increase the heat to high and bring to a boil; decrease the heat and simmer until the chicken is done, about 10 minutes.

Serve this chili with fresh chopped tomatoes, green onions, and nonfat sour cream on top.

HEARTY VEGETABLE LENTIL SOUP

MAKES 6 1½-CUP SERVINGS

5 cups nonfat, low-sodium chicken or vegetable broth
2 stalks celery, chopped
1 medium onion, chopped
1 green bell pepper, seeded and chopped
1 red bell pepper, seeded and chopped
1 large carrot, scraped and chopped
2 medium cloves garlic, minced
1 cup dry lentils, rinsed
1 medium zucchini, washed and diced
3 medium red-skinned potatoes, washed and diced
½ cup no-salt-added tomato sauce
1 cup no-salt-added diced tomatoes
½ tsp. curry powder
½ tsp. dried basil

NUTRITION
INFORMATION

Each serving contains
approximately:
240 calories
14 g protein
43 g carbohydrate
2 g total fat
3 mg cholesterol
132 mg sodium
13 g dietary fiber
8% calories from fat

Caloric Density: 240

Combine the broth, celery, onion, bell pepper, carrot, garlic, and lentils in a large saucepan or soup pot. Bring to a boil, reduce heat and simmer, partially covered, for 30 to 40 minutes.

Add the zucchini, potatoes, tomato sauce, diced tomatoes, curry powder, and basil. Mix thoroughly and simmer, partially covered, about 15 minutes, or until potatoes are tender.

ITALIAN VEGETABLE STEW

MAKES 6 1½-CUP SERVINGS

½ cup white wine
1 medium onion, sliced
2 cloves garlic, peeled and crushed
2 celery stalks, sliced crosswise
2 medium red-skinned potatoes, cut into 1-inch dice
1 tsp. finely chopped fresh rosemary (or ½ tsp. dried)
small pinch of saffron (optional)
¼ cup nonfat, low-sodium,
    chicken or vegetable broth, plus extra as needed
1 Tbs. lite soy sauce
1 Tbs. Worcestershire sauce
1 Tbs. balsamic vinegar
1 small (or half large) eggplant,
    seeded and cut into 1-inch cubes
1 red bell pepper, seeded and cut into strips
1 yellow bell pepper, seeded and cut into strips
¼ tsp. dried red pepper flakes
3 or 4 medium tomatoes, seeded and cut into chunks
1½ cups cooked white beans (or salt-free, drained, canned beans)
2 Tbs. chopped fresh basil leaves
cracked pepper, to taste
2 Tbs. chopped fresh parsley

NUTRITION INFORMATION

Each serving contains approximately:
178 calories
7 g protein
35 g carbohydrate
less than 1 g total fat
0 mg cholesterol
213 mg sodium
7.8 g dietary fiber
4% calories from fat

Caloric Density: 210

Pour the wine into a large skillet, add the onion and garlic and cook, covered, over medium heat for 2 minutes. Stir in the celery, potatoes, rosemary, and saffron, if using, until well mixed and golden. Cook, covered, over medium heat, stirring occasionally, about 10 minutes, adding a little chicken or vegetable broth if it becomes too dry.

Combine the ¼ cup broth, soy sauce, Worcestershire sauce, and balsamic vinegar and add it to the skillet along with the eggplant, peppers, and pepper flakes. Cook for another 10 minutes, or until the vegetables are tender. Add the tomatoes, cook for another 2 to 3 minutes then stir in the white beans, basil and a sprinkling of black pepper, if desired. Mix well and cook until the beans are heated through. Sprinkle with chopped parsley and serve either warm or at room temperature.

Use as a vegetarian main dish, side dish, or as a topping for rice or pasta (pasta primavera).

JAMAICAN FISH STEW

MAKES 6 1½-CUP SERVINGS
(1 cup stew, ½ cup rice)

2 cups peeled, cubed winter squash
   (acorn, butternut, yams, etc.)
2 cups diced tomatoes (fresh or no-salt-added canned)
1 Tbs. fresh lime juice
1 clove garlic, minced
1 Tbs. lite soy sauce
¼ cup dry white wine
¾ lb. cubed, firm, white fish
   (orange roughy, halibut, sea bass, etc.)

NUTRITION
INFORMATION

Each serving contains
approximately:
205 calories
15 g protein
31 g carbohydrate
1.6 g total fat
14 mg cholesterol
174 mg sodium
3.4 g dietary fiber
7% calories from fat

Caloric Density: 319

Put the squash, tomatoes, lime juice, garlic, soy sauce, and white wine into an 11-inch skillet. Simmer, covered, over medium-low heat for 15 minutes, or until squash is tender.

Add the fish. Simmer 5 to 6 minutes, covered, or until the fish is cooked through.

Serve the stew on a bed of hot brown rice, garnished with a sprinkling of chopped green onions.

SPLIT PEA SOUP

MAKES 6 1¼-CUP SERVINGS

5 cups nonfat, low-sodium chicken or
    vegetable stock (more if necessary)
1½ cups green or yellow split peas
1 small onion, chopped
1 small leek, chopped (white part only)
2 cloves garlic
1 large carrot, diced
2 stalks celery, sliced
1 tsp. dried thyme
1 bay leaf
1 Tbs. lite soy sauce
2 Tbs. natural rice vinegar

NUTRITION
INFORMATION

Each serving contains
approximately:
117 calories
7 g protein
18 g carbohydrate
1.6 g total fat
0 mg cholesterol
215 mg sodium
5.4 g dietary fiber
13% calories from fat

Caloric Density: 167

In a soup pot or Dutch oven, combine the chicken broth, split peas, onion, leek, and garlic. Simmer, covered, about 30 minutes. Add the carrot, celery, thyme, bay leaf, and soy sauce and simmer, covered, an additional 30 minutes. Add more broth if the soup becomes too thick. Stir in the rice vinegar and serve hot.

A creamier soup may be obtained by puréeing the soup in two batches in a food processor.

VEGETABLE BARLEY STEW

MAKES 6 2-CUP SERVINGS

vegetable oil cooking spray
1 cup chopped onion
1 clove garlic, minced
1/2 cup chopped celery
1 15-ounce can diced no-salt-added tomatoes
2 cups water
2 cups nonfat, low-sodium chicken broth
1 potato, peeled and diced
3 carrots, peeled and diced
3/4 cup pearled barley
1/3 cup tomato paste
1/2 tsp. dried thyme
black pepper, to taste

Garnish: 3 Tbs. chopped fresh parsley

NUTRITION INFORMATION

Each serving contains approximately:
247 calories
10 g protein
50 g carbohydrate
less than 1 g total fat
0 mg cholesterol
166 mg sodium
10 g dietary fiber
3% calories from fat

Caloric Density: 214

Spray a 4- to 6-quart Dutch oven generously with vegetable oil cooking spray and heat over medium-high heat. Sauté the onion and garlic until golden, about 3 minutes. Add the rest of the ingredients and bring to a boil. Reduce heat to low and simmer until the barley is tender, about 45 minutes.

Ladle into large soup bowls. Garnish each serving with 1/2 tablespoon of chopped parsley.

WINTER SQUASH STEW

MAKES 6 1½-CUP SERVINGS

1 medium onion, diced
2 large cloves garlic
1 tsp. dried thyme
¼ cup low-sodium, nonfat chicken or vegetable broth
4 cups mixed winter squash,
    peeled and cut into 1-inch pieces*
4 medium red potatoes,
    scrubbed and cut into 1-inch pieces
2 stalks celery, cut in 1-inch pieces
1½ cups low-sodium tomato or V-8 juice
2 Tbs. balsamic vinegar
½ cup red wine
2 bay leaves
1 Tbs. lite soy sauce
1 Tbs. Worcestershire sauce
1½ cups string beans, peeled and cut in 2-inch pieces
1 large zucchini, scrubbed and sliced
1 8-ounce can no-salt-added garbanzo beans, drained
1 cup water or extra broth (if needed)
½ cup chopped fresh parsley

*Choose from butternut, yam, acorn, or banana squash.

NUTRITION
INFORMATION

Each serving contains
approximately:
212 calories
7 g protein
42 g carbohydrate
less than 1 g total fat
0 mg cholesterol
161 mg sodium
7 g dietary fiber
3% calories from fat

Caloric Density: 239

In a 6-quart stew pot or Dutch oven, cook the onion, garlic, and thyme together in the broth, over low heat, for about 3 minutes.

Add the mixed winter squash, red potatoes, celery, tomato juice, balsamic vinegar, red wine, bay leaves, soy sauce, and Worcestershire sauce. Bring to a boil, cover the pot and reduce the heat. Simmer over medium-low heat for about 20 minutes. Check the liquid and, if it is beginning to look too dry, add up to 1 cup of water or extra broth, if necessary.

Add the string beans and zucchini and cook for 10 minutes more. Add the garbanzo beans and cook until the beans are heated through.

Sprinkle with chopped parsley and serve hot.

ANGEL HAIR PASTA WITH TOMATO BASIL SAUCE

MAKES 4 1½-CUP SERVINGS

3 large ripe tomatoes, cored and sliced
½ cup onions, chopped
3 tsp. minced garlic
1 cup sweet bell peppers, diced
vegetable oil cooking spray
½ cup fresh basil leaves
ground black pepper, to taste
6 Tbs. tomato paste
¼ cup nonfat, low-sodium chicken broth
8 ounces angel hair pasta or thin spaghetti
2 Tbs. fat-free Parmesan cheese

NUTRITION
INFORMATION

Each serving contains
approximately:
233 calories
8 g protein
48 g carbohydrate
1.5 g total fat
0 mg cholesterol
99 mg sodium
5.5 g dietary fiber
6% calories from fat

Caloric Density: 313

Place oven rack close to the top of the oven and preheat broiler. Place tomatoes, onions, garlic, and peppers on large baking tray in a single layer. Spray them lightly with vegetable oil cooking spray. Broil veggies until golden brown and tender, about 15 minutes.

Place broiled veggies, basil leaves, pepper, tomato paste, and broth in a food processor or blender and purée until smooth.

Cook pasta according to package directions; drain in colander.

Reheat sauce in microwave or on stovetop and toss with the cooked pasta. Serve hot, topping each serving with ½ tablespoon Parmesan cheese.

ASIAN SPICY NOODLES WITH TOFU AND SPINACH

MAKES 2 SERVINGS

1 10-ounce bag leaf spinach
vegetable oil cooking spray
4 cloves garlic
2 Tbs. chopped fresh ginger
1/4 cup nonfat low-sodium chicken or vegetable broth
1/4 cup dry sherry
1 Tbs. lite soy sauce
1 Tbs. Worcestershire sauce
1 Tbs. balsamic vinegar
1/4 tsp. Chinese five-spice seasoning
2 tsp. cornstarch
2 Tbs. cold water
4 ounces firm tofu, cut into 1/2-inch cubes
1/4 lb. whole-wheat spaghetti, broken in half
4 scallions, cut into thin strips about 3 inches long,
    including green tops

NUTRITION
INFORMATION

Each serving contains
approximately:
72 calories
3 g protein
13 g carbohydrate
less than 1 g total fat
0 mg cholesterol
81 mg sodium
1.6 g dietary fiber
7% calories from fat

Caloric Density: 454

Steam spinach until just tender. Drain, coarsely chop, and set aside.

Spray a small saucepan or skillet with vegetable oil cooking spray. Add the garlic and ginger and sauté 1 to 2 minutes. Stir in the broth, sherry, soy sauce, Worcestershire sauce, balsamic vinegar, and five-spice seasoning. Bring to a simmer over medium heat. Combine the cornstarch and water and stir into the sauce. Simmer until thickened and clear. Add the tofu cubes and stir gently to coat well. Remove from heat and set aside.

Cook pasta until al dente and drain. Reheat the sauce and tofu until just hot. Pour it over the pasta, add the spinach and scallions and toss gently until well mixed. Serve hot.

Note: Additional vegetables such as lightly steamed snow peas, green beans, and sliced water chestnuts may be added to this dish. The extra vegetables will also lower the caloric density.

BARBECUED PORTABELLA MUSHROOMS

MAKES 2 1-CUP SERVINGS

8 ounces portabella mushrooms
    (about 3 medium mushrooms)

Sauce:
1 cup no-added-salt tomato sauce
1 Tbs. balsamic vinegar
1 Tbs. molasses
$\frac{1}{2}$ tsp. chili powder
2 tsp. Worcestershire sauce
1 tsp. lite soy sauce
1 Tbs. fresh lemon juice
$\frac{1}{2}$ tsp. garlic powder
$\frac{1}{2}$ tsp. onion powder

NUTRITION
INFORMATION

Each serving contains
approximately:
123 calories
6.5 g protein
24 g carbohydrate
0.5 g total fat
0 mg cholesterol
196 mg sodium
6 g dietary fiber
4% calories from fat

Caloric Density: 203

Wash the mushrooms with cold water to remove loose dirt. Drain on paper towels while preparing the sauce.

Combine all the sauce ingredients in a medium microwave-safe bowl. Stir well. Add the mushrooms into the sauce and turn them so they are coated on both sides. Microwave the mushrooms until tender, about 8 minutes.

To serve: cut in slices and serve with the sauce. Serve them over salad, rice or pasta. They can be served warm or chilled.

BROCCOLI CHEESE POTATOES

MAKES 2 SERVINGS

2 medium baking potatoes
³/₄ cup nonfat ricotta cheese
¹/₄ cup nonfat sour cream
1 Tbs. fat-free Parmesan cheese
¹/₄ cup chopped green onion
¹/₂ tsp. dried oregano
ground black pepper, to taste
2 cups steamed broccoli
2 Tbs. shredded low-fat mozzarella cheese

NUTRITION
INFORMATION

Each serving contains
approximately:
383 calories
25 g protein
69 g carbohydrate
1 g total fat
8.5 mg cholesterol
356 mg sodium
8 g dietary fiber
3% calories from fat

Caloric Density: 393

Wash potatoes in cold water and dry with paper towels. Pierce with a fork. Microwave potatoes for 4 minutes, turn over and microwave until tender, about 2 more minutes.

Meanwhile, mix the ricotta cheese with sour cream, Parmesan, green onion and spices in a medium mixing bowl. Steam broccoli until tender.

Cut baked potatoes open with a knife and place on a microwave-safe plate. Fluff insides with a fork and fill with the ricotta mixture. Top each half with 1 cup steamed broccoli and 1 tablespoon mozzarella cheese. Microwave for 30 seconds. Serve hot with a large tossed salad.

ORANGE RICE PILAF

MAKES 6 1-CUP SERVINGS

¹/₄ cup orange juice
1 cup chopped red onion
1 cup sliced celery
¹/₂ cup diced red pepper
shredded peel of two oranges (use a zester, or remove
    peel with a peeler and shred with a sharp knife)
¹/₄ tsp. ground black pepper
1 Tbs. lite soy sauce
2 Tbs. balsamic vinegar
1¹/₂ cups cooked brown rice (¹/₂ cup raw)
1¹/₂ cups cooked wild rice (¹/₂ cup raw)
1 cup orange segments, transparent
    skin removed (or 8-ounce can mandarin
    oranges packed in juice)
2 Tbs. natural rice vinegar (optional)

NUTRITION
INFORMATION

Each serving contains
approximately:
141 calories
4 g protein
30 g carbohydrate
less than 1 g total fat
0 mg cholesterol
123 mg sodium
3.5 g dietary fiber
5% calories from fat

Caloric Density: 327

Pour the orange juice into a large skillet, add the red onion and celery and cook, covered, over medium heat for 2 minutes. Add the red pepper and cook for 1 minute more. Stir in the orange peel, black pepper, soy sauce, and balsamic vinegar.

Turn the heat to medium low and add the cooked rices. Stir until well combined and the rice is heated through. Gently mix in the orange segments. Taste the rice and add the optional rice vinegar, if needed.

Serve hot as a side dish with poultry, fish, or pork tenderloin, or serve chilled or at room temperature as a rice salad.

OVEN-BAKED BEANS

MAKES 6 1½-CUP SERVINGS

8 ounces dried pinto beans
3 cups cold water
3 cups nonfat, low-sodium chicken broth
1 cup water
½ cup no-salt-added ketchup
¼ cup molasses
1 cup diced onion
2 cups peeled and diced sweet potatoes
1 cup diced green pepper
pinch of ground cloves
½ tsp. dried thyme
ground black pepper, to taste
1½ Tbs. lite soy sauce

NUTRITION
INFORMATION

Each serving contains
approximately:
272 calories
13 g protein
54 g carbohydrate
0.5 g total fat
0 mg cholesterol
246 mg sodium
11.5 g dietary fiber
3% calories from fat

Caloric Density: 325

Place the beans in a large container and add the 3 cups cold water. Refrigerate overnight. Drain and rinse. Note: For quicker soaking, place the beans in a pot, cover with 3 cups water, cover and bring to a boil; remove from the heat and allow to stand 1 hour. Drain and discard the water before proceeding.

Preheat oven to 350°. Place the beans and all the remaining ingredients into a large ovenproof Dutch oven and heat on top of the stove over high heat. Bring to a boil, stir well and cover. Place the Dutch oven in the middle of the oven and allow to cook until the beans and sweet potatoes are tender, about 1½ hours. Serve hot.

POTATO, TOMATO, AND LEEK TERRINE

MAKES 6 SERVINGS

vegetable oil cooking spray
3 medium baking potatoes, peeled and sliced thin
2 cups sliced leeks (white part only)
3 medium tomatoes, sliced
1 Tbs. chopped basil
1 Tbs. minced garlic
$1/2$ cup nonfat, low-sodium chicken or vegetable broth
$1^1/2$ tsp. lite soy sauce
$1/8$ tsp. ground black pepper

NUTRITION
INFORMATION

Each serving contains
approximately:
64 calories
2 g protein
14 g carbohydrate
less than 1 g total fat
0 mg cholesterol
68 mg sodium
1.3 g dietary fiber
5% calories from fat

Caloric Density: 249

Preheat oven to 350°. Coat an 8-inch-square baking pan with vegetable oil cooking spray.

Alternately layer the potatoes, leeks, and tomatoes in the baking pan, sprinkling some basil and garlic between the layers, ending with a layer of potatoes. Combine the broth, soy sauce, and pepper and add the mixture to the terrine.

Cover with foil and bake for 1 hour, or until potatoes are tender. Uncover the pan and cook for 10 minutes more, or until the top is golden and slightly crisp.

Serve hot or at room temperature, as a side dish, or a vegetarian main dish with additional vegetables and a salad.

RATATOUILLE

MAKES 4 ½-CUP SERVINGS

2 cups diced eggplant
⅔ cup chopped red onion
1 tsp. minced garlic
1 cup diced zucchini
⅓ cup red wine
⅔ cup diced tomatoes
¼ cup low-sodium V-8 juice
1 Tbs. balsamic vinegar
½ tsp. crushed, dried oregano
¼ tsp. hot pepper flakes
1½ Tbs. chopped fresh basil

NUTRITION
INFORMATION

Each serving contains
approximately:
67 calories
2 g protein
11 g carbohydrate
less than 1 g total fat
0 mg cholesterol
20 mg sodium
2.9 g dietary fiber
6% calories from fat

Caloric Density: 149

In a large skillet over medium heat, simmer the eggplant, red onion, garlic, and zucchini in the red wine, covered, for about 10 minutes, stirring frequently. Add the tomatoes, V-8 juice, balsamic vinegar, oregano, hot pepper flakes, and basil. Mix well and simmer for 5 minutes, covered. Remove the lid and if the mixture is too liquid simmer for an additional 5 minutes uncovered.

Serve hot, cold, or at room temperature as a vegetable side dish for fish or poultry, or use as a topping for whole-wheat rice or pasta.

SHIITAKE MUSHROOM RISOTTO

MAKES 6 1-CUP SERVINGS

2 cups cooked wild rice
2 cups cooked brown rice
²/₃ cup chopped onions
¹/₂ cup chopped celery
²/₃ cup chopped red bell peppers
¹/₄ cup white wine
3 cups sliced shiitake mushrooms
1 bay leaf
¹/₄ tsp. dried thyme
2 cups chopped tomatoes
    (or 1 16-ounce can diced, no-salt-added tomatoes)
2 Tbs. balsamic vinegar
¹/₄ tsp. black pepper
1 Tbs. lite soy sauce
1 Tbs. Worcestershire sauce
¹/₂ tsp. dried oregano
4 Tbs. chopped fresh basil
¹/₂ cup nonfat, low-sodium broth or water
    (more if necessary)
¹/₄ cup chopped fresh parsley

NUTRITION
INFORMATION

Each serving contains
approximately:
210 calories
6 g protein
43 g carbohydrate
1.3 g total fat
0 mg cholesterol
176 mg sodium
5 g dietary fiber
6% calories from fat

Caloric Density: 287

Cook wild and brown rices separately according to package directions. You will need ²/₃ cup dry rice and 1¹/₃ cups water to yield 2 cups cooked rice.

In a large skillet, over medium-low heat, cook the onions, celery, and bell peppers in the white wine until the wine has evaporated. Add the shiitake mushrooms, bay leaf, thyme, tomatoes, and balsamic vinegar. Cover the pan and cook over medium heat for about 5 minutes, or until the mushrooms are softened. Stir in the pepper, soy sauce, Worcestershire sauce, oregano, basil, and wild and brown rice.

Continue to cook and stir, adding broth or water, if necessary, until everything is combined and well heated through. Mix in the chopped parsley and serve.

Serve as a side dish with chicken or fish, or as a vegetarian main course with steamed or grilled mixed vegetables.

TOMATO-CARROT LASAGNA

MAKES 8 1½-CUP SERVINGS

olive oil cooking spray
2 cups carrots, peeled and thinly sliced
1 cup chopped onions
2 tsp. minced garlic
3 15-ounce cans diced, no-salt-added tomatoes
1 6-ounce can tomato paste
1 tsp. dried oregano
2 cups fat-free ricotta cheese
¼ cup sliced green onions
1 tsp. Italian seasoning
15 dry lasagna noodles (10 ounces)
1 cup shredded low-fat mozzarella cheese

NUTRITION
INFORMATION

Each serving contains
approximately:
290 calories
20 g protein
50 g carbohydrate
1.5 g total fat
5 mg cholesterol
289 mg sodium
5.5 g dietary fiber
5% calories from fat

Caloric Density: 360

Generously spray a Dutch oven with olive oil cooking spray and heat over medium-high heat. Sauté the carrots, onions, and garlic until golden brown, about 3 minutes. Add the canned tomatoes with the juice and tomato paste. Bring to a boil then lower to a simmer. Cook until the carrots are tender, about 8 minutes. Add the oregano.

Make the ricotta cheese filling by mixing the ricotta with the green onions and Italian seasoning together in a medium mixing bowl.

Preheat oven to 350°. Place 1 cup of sauce in a large 9 by 13-inch oven-proof glass baking dish. Add 5 dry uncooked lasagna noodles, overlapping slightly. Spread the noodles with 1 cup of ricotta filling then cover with sauce. Follow with noodles, ricotta, sauce, noodles and finally a layer of sauce. Cover with foil and bake for 1 hour; remove from oven.

Top with shredded mozzarella, cover with foil and allow to sit on top of the stove for 10 minutes. Remove foil and cut in to 8 squares. Serve hot.

Note: the carrot-tomato sauce is also great over penne, rigatoni, shells, or other short, tube-shaped pasta.

TWO-PEPPER RISOTTO

MAKES 4 1½-CUP SERVINGS

1 red bell pepper, diced
1 green bell pepper, diced
1 tomato, diced
½ onion, diced
1 tsp. minced garlic
1 cup arborio rice
5 cups nonfat, low-sodium chicken broth
1 Tbs. chopped fresh basil
ground black pepper, to taste
2 Tbs. fat-free Parmesan cheese

NUTRITION
INFORMATION

Each serving contains
approximately:
294 calories
13 g protein
53 g carbohydrate
1 g total fat
2 mg cholesterol
265 mg sodium
3 g dietary fiber
3% calories from fat

Caloric Density: 245

Preheat broiler and position rack at the top of the oven. Spread peppers, tomato, onion, and garlic on a large baking sheet. Broil until golden brown, about 15 minutes. Stir occasionally.

Combine broiled vegetables with rice and 2 cups broth in a large Dutch oven and place over medium-high heat. Cover and bring to a boil. Stir frequently and continue cooking uncovered. As the broth evaporates, add more in 1-cup increments. Cook until the rice is tender and most of the broth is absorbed, about 35 minutes. (Alternatively, you can add roasted veggies, rice, and all the broth at once in a large microwaveable container, cover and microwave on high for 35 minutes.) Stir well and add fresh basil, black pepper, to taste, and Parmesan cheese. Allow to stand for a few minutes and serve. This dish goes well with steamed vegetables or a large tossed salad.

VEGGIE KABOBS WITH GARLIC TERIYAKI SAUCE

MAKES 4 SERVINGS

3 cups cooked brown rice
8 large bamboo skewers
1 cup large mushrooms (8)
$^1/_2$ large eggplant, cut into large cubes
1 medium onion, cut into large cubes
8 cherry tomatoes, stems removed
1 green pepper, cut into large cubes

Marinade:
2 Tbs. lite soy sauce
$^1/_4$ cup fresh orange juice
2 Tbs. water
1 tsp. sesame oil
2 tsp. grated fresh ginger root
2 tsp. minced garlic

NUTRITION
INFORMATION

Each serving contains
approximately:
239 calories
7 g protein
47 g carbohydrate
3 g total fat
0 mg cholesterol
267 mg sodium
5.5 g dietary fiber
12% calories from fat

Caloric Density: 303

Cook brown rice according to package directions. For 3 cups of cooked brown rice you need 1 cup of uncooked rice and 2 cups of water.

Soak bamboo skewers in water. Make marinade by combining all marinade ingredients in a medium bowl. Par cook the eggplant, onions, mushrooms, and green pepper together in a covered container in the microwave, until crisp-tender, about 4 minutes. Rinse them with cool water to stop further cooking.

Place all of the vegetables on the skewers and place the kabobs in a large shallow pan. Pour the marinade over the top, cover and refrigerate. Allow to marinate for at least 15 minutes or several hours.

Preheat the oven broiler or prepare the grill. Broil or grill the vegetable kabobs until golden, brushing a few times with the marinade. Serve hot with 2 kabobs and $^3/_4$ cup brown rice per person.

BAKED HALIBUT WITH ORANGE-PEACH GLAZE

MAKES 4 SERVINGS

4 4-ounce fresh halibut fillets
vegetable oil cooking spray
$\frac{1}{2}$ cup diced onion
2 peaches, pitted and diced (leave skin on)
$\frac{1}{2}$ cup orange juice
pinch of ground allspice
1 tsp. lite soy sauce

NUTRITION
INFORMATION

Each serving contains
approximately:
137 calories
21 g protein
10 g carbohydrate
1 g total fat
48 mg cholesterol
107 mg sodium
1.5 g dietary fiber
6% calories from fat

Caloric Density: 289

Preheat oven to 350°. Place fish fillets in large glass or ceramic ovenproof baking dish.

Lightly spray a nonstick skillet with vegetable oil cooking spray and heat over medium-high heat. Sauté the onion until golden brown then add the peaches, orange juice, allspice, and soy sauce. Bring to a boil and cook briefly, about 2 minutes. Pour the sauce over the fish and place in the oven. Bake the fish until it is done and fork-tender, about 10 minutes. Serve the fish immediately with the sauce spooned over the top of each piece.

Try serving this dish with your favorite steamed vegetables and boiled new potatoes.

BAKED RASPBERRY CHICKEN

MAKES 4 SERVINGS (including ½ cup of sauce)

4 boneless skinless chicken breast halves
vegetable oil cooking spray
½ cup chopped onions
2 cups frozen unsweetened raspberries
1 cup diced stewed no-salt-added tomatoes
2 Tbs. water
pinch of ground cinnamon
½ tsp. dried thyme

NUTRITION
INFORMATION

Each serving contains
approximately:
200 calories
27 g protein
12 g carbohydrate
4 g total fat
72 mg cholesterol
178 mg sodium
5 g dietary fiber
18% calories from fat

Caloric Density: 439

With ½ cup brown
rice and 1 cup
steamed broccoli

Calorie Density: 385

Preheat oven to 350°. Place chicken breast halves in large glass baking dish.
    Lightly spray a large nonstick skillet with vegetable oil cooking spray and heat over medium-high heat. Sauté the onions until they are golden, about 3 minutes. Add the raspberries, tomatoes, water, and seasonings. Bring the raspberry sauce to a boil and cook for 1 minute. Pour the sauce over the chicken and place the chicken in the oven. Bake uncovered until the chicken is done, about 15 to 20 minutes. Serve hot with the sauce spooned over each chicken breast.

CABBAGE ROLLS

MAKES 4 SERVINGS

vegetable oil cooking spray
$\frac{1}{2}$ cup chopped onion
$\frac{1}{2}$ cup chopped mushrooms
1 tsp. minced garlic
$\frac{1}{2}$ cup chopped tomatoes
$\frac{1}{8}$ tsp. black pepper
2 Tbs. chopped fresh parsley
1 Tbs. lite soy sauce
$1\frac{1}{2}$ tsp. Worcestershire sauce
$\frac{1}{4}$ tsp. curry powder
$1\frac{1}{2}$ cups cooked brown rice
4 large cabbage leaves, steamed until just limp
$1\frac{1}{4}$ cups low-sodium tomato or marinara sauce

NUTRITION
INFORMATION

Each serving contains
approximately:
128 calories
4.6 g protein
26 g carbohydrate
1.3 g total fat
0 mg cholesterol
177 mg sodium
3.7 g dietary fiber
9% calories from fat

Caloric Density: 238

Heat a medium, nonstick skillet until just hot and spray with vegetable oil cooking spray. Add the onions, mushrooms, and garlic and cook over medium-low heat, covered, about 5 minutes. Add the tomatoes, pepper, and parsely and cook a minute or two longer, stirring. Mix in the soy sauce, Worcestershire sauce, and curry powder. Transfer the mixture to a large bowl. Add the cooked rice and mix well.

Lay the steamed cabbage leaves out flat. Spoon $\frac{1}{4}$ of the rice mixture into the center of each leaf. Fold each cabbage leaf envelope style over the mixture to form a tight package.

Spread $\frac{1}{4}$ cup of the tomato sauce over the bottom of a baking dish, just large enough to hold the four cabbage rolls. Lay the rolls in the dish and cover with the rest of the tomato sauce. Bake, covered, at 350° for 20 minutes. Serve hot with mashed or baked potatoes and fresh, steamed vegetables.

CHICKEN AND VEGETABLE CURRY

MAKES 6 SERVINGS

½ cup dry white wine
1 lb. skinless chicken breast, cut into 1½-inch chunks
1 cup chopped red onion
2 cloves garlic, minced
1 cup sliced carrot
1 cup sliced celery
½ red bell pepper, diced
1 cup sliced mushrooms
1 large zucchini, washed and diced
2 Tbs. cornstarch
1½ cups nonfat, low-sodium chicken broth
2 tsp. mild curry powder
1 Tbs. lite soy sauce
1 Tbs. white wine Worcestershire sauce
⅔ cup nonfat milk powder
½ cup frozen peas

NUTRITION
INFORMATION

Each serving contains
approximately:
236 calories
29 g protein
17 g carbohydrate
3.7 g total fat
66 mg cholesterol
287 mg sodium
3 g dietary fiber
14% calories from fat

Caloric Density: 360

Pour the wine into a large skillet set over medium heat, add the chicken pieces and cook, turning the pieces, until the chicken is just white. Remove the chicken with a slotted spoon and set aside.

Add the onion and garlic to the pan (adding a little more wine, if necessary) and cook for 2 minutes. Add the carrot, celery, red bell pepper, and mushrooms, and cook for a few minutes, stirring occasionally. Add the zucchini and cook for 1 to 2 minutes more.

Dissolve the cornstarch in the chicken broth. Stir in the curry powder, soy sauce, white wine Worcestershire sauce, and the milk powder, and mix until smooth. Add the mixture to the vegetables in the skillet a little at a time, stirring until the liquid thickens a little. Add the cooked chicken pieces and the peas. Cook and stir until the curry is thick and creamy and the chicken and peas are heated through.

Serve over brown rice.

FISH FILLETS WITH PINEAPPLE-LIME SALSA

MAKES 2 SERVINGS

¹/₃ cup unsweetened pineapple juice
1 Tbs. fresh lime juice
2 to 3 Tbs. salsa (Enrico's unsalted Chunky Salsa
  is a good choice)
vegetable oil cooking spray
2 5-ounce fish fillets
  (orange roughy, sole, halibut, etc.)
¹/₂ cup white flour (only part will be used)
2 Tbs. chopped green onions

NUTRITION
INFORMATION

Each serving contains
approximately:
216 calories
29 g protein
20 g carbohydrate
1.4 g total fat
28 mg cholesterol
176 mg sodium
less than 1 g dietary
fiber
6% calories from fat

Caloric Density: 419

In a small bowl, combine the pineapple and lime juices and the salsa and set aside. Dry the fish fillets thoroughly with paper towels.

Spray a small nonstick skillet with vegetable oil cooking spray and put the pan over high heat. Dredge the fish fillets with flour, shaking off the excess, and sauté the fillets on one side until they are lightly browned (2 to 3 minutes). *Don't move the fish around while it is browning or it will stick.* Using two spatulas, gently turn the fillets over and brown for 2 minutes on the other side. Remove the pan from the heat and allow it to cool off a little before continuing.

Stir up the pineapple-lime salsa and pour it over the fish. Lower the heat to medium low and cook for 4 to 5 minutes, basting with the sauce once in a while, until the fish is cooked through and the sauce has been reduced to a thick glaze.

Garnish with a sprinkling of green onions and serve.

GARLIC BROILED SEA BASS WITH GRAPE SALSA

MAKES 4 SERVINGS (1 fillet plus ½ cup of salsa)

4 4-ounce sea bass fillets
2 tsp. minced garlic
juice of 1 lemon

Salsa:
1 cup seedless red grapes,
    sliced or cut into quarters
½ cup diced fresh tomato
½ cup sliced green onion
dash of hot pepper sauce
1 tsp. chopped fresh cilantro
juice of half a lemon

NUTRITION
INFORMATION

Each serving contains
approximately:
142 calories
21 g protein
8 g carbohydrate
2.5 g total fat
46 mg cholesterol
83 mg sodium
1 g dietary fiber
16% calories from fat

Caloric Density: 331

Preheat oven to 375°. Remove any visible bones from the sea bass fillets and place them on a baking sheet so they do not touch. Mix the minced garlic and lemon juice in a small bowl; rub it over the fish. Bake the fish until it is done and fork-tender, about 20 minutes.

To make the Grape Salsa, combine the salsa ingredients in a small mixing bowl and chill until ready to serve.

Serve the fish hot from the oven with ½ cup of salsa on top of each fillet.

GINGER SHRIMP STIR-FRY

MAKES 4 1½-CUP SERVINGS

3 cups cooked brown rice
vegetable oil cooking spray
1 Tbs. minced garlic
1 Tbs. fresh grated ginger
1 cup sliced carrots
1 cup sliced green peppers
1 cup broccoli florets
2 cups shredded bok choy or cabbage
½ cup sliced green onion
½ cup nonfat, low-sodium chicken broth
1 Tbs. cornstarch
12 ounces peeled and deveined shrimp,
    cut into chunks
1 Tbs. lite soy sauce
1 Tbs. Worcestershire sauce
1 tsp. sesame oil
dash of cayenne pepper

NUTRITION
INFORMATION

Each serving contains
approximately:
320 calories
24 g protein
46 g carbohydrate
4 g total fat
129 mg cholesterol
374 mg sodium
5.5 g dietary fiber
12% calories from fat

Caloric Density: 353

Cook brown rice according to package directions. For 3 cups cooked rice you need 1 cup uncooked brown rice and 2 cups of water.

Meanwhile, spray a large nonstick skillet with vegetable oil cooking spray and heat over medium-high heat. Sauté the garlic until lightly browned, about 45 seconds. Add the ginger, carrots, and green peppers. Continue cooking until the vegetables begin to soften, about 3 minutes. Add the broccoli, bok choy, and green onion and continue cooking. Mix the chicken broth and the cornstarch together in a small bowl and add to the pan, stirring constantly. Add the shrimp, soy sauce, Worcestershire sauce, sesame oil, and cayenne pepper. Cook and stir until the shrimp is done, about 2 minutes.

Serve the Ginger Shrimp Stir-Fry over the brown rice.

HONEY-MUSTARD ROASTED CHICKEN AND VEGETABLES

MAKES 4 2-CUP SERVINGS

2 cups sliced zucchini
1 cup sliced carrots
2 cups sliced cauliflower
1 cup chopped onion
4 3½-ounce boneless skinless
    chicken breast halves
1 tsp. minced garlic
2 Tbs. honey
1 Tbs. stone ground mustard
2 Tbs. red wine vinegar

NUTRITION
INFORMATION

Each serving contains
approximately:
195 calories
25.5 g protein
20 g carbohydrate
1.5 g total fat
57 mg cholesterol
125 mg sodium
3.5 g dietary fiber
8% calories from fat

Caloric Density: 328

Preheat oven to 350°. Place vegetables in large glass or ceramic ovenproof baking dish. Arrange chicken breasts on top of the vegetables.

Mix the garlic, honey, mustard and vinegar in a small mixing bowl. Smear the mixture over top of each chicken breast.

Cover the dish with foil and place in the oven; bake for 10 minutes; uncover and bake until done, about 10 to 15 minutes. Remove chicken breasts and stir vegetables well. Slice chicken breasts on the bias and serve over the vegetables.

"PAN-FRIED" FISH FILLETS WITH LEMON BUTTER

MAKES 4 SERVINGS

1½ lbs. white fish fillets
    (orange roughy, halibut, sole, etc.)
½ cup white flour (only part will be used)
1 tsp. lemon-pepper seasoning
vegetable oil cooking spray
nonfat butter-spray ("I Can't Believe It's Not Butter")
½ fresh lemon
2 Tbs. chopped fresh parsley

NUTRITION
INFORMATION

Each serving contains approximately:
185 calories
33 g protein
8 g carbohydrate
1.6 g total fat
44 mg cholesterol
259 mg sodium
less than 1 g dietary fiber
8% calories from fat

Caloric Density: 430

Dry the fish pieces thoroughly with paper towels. Mix the flour and lemon-pepper seasoning together and spread it on a large plate. Heat a large, nonstick skillet over medium heat and spray with vegetable oil cooking spray.

Dredge each piece of fish in the flour mixture, shaking off the excess, and lay them in the pan. Cook over medium-high heat. Do not move the fish around. When the fillets have browned on one side (3 to 4 minutes) turn each piece, using two spatulas. Lower the heat to medium and brown on the other side (3 to 4 minutes). The fish should be cooked through (test for doneness by cutting into the thickest piece). Lightly spray the fish with butter-spray, and then a squeeze of fresh lemon juice. Sprinkle with chopped parsely and serve.

Serve with boiled new potatoes, fresh steamed vegetables, and additional lemon slices.

POACHED SALMON IN VEGETABLE DILL SAUCE

MAKES 4 SERVINGS

1¼ lb. salmon fillet, skin removed
2 stalks celery, diced
1 medium red onion, diced
1 cup coarsely chopped fresh parsley
1 cup nonfat, low-sodium chicken or vegetable broth
1 cup dry white wine
1 tsp. lite soy sauce
1 Tbs. white wine Worcestershire sauce
1 cup plain nonfat yogurt
1 Tbs. chopped fresh dill (or 1 tsp. dried)
1 tsp. no-salt-added Dijon mustard
½ tsp. dried tarragon

NUTRITION
INFORMATION

Each serving contains
approximately:
270 calories
37 g protein
11 g carbohydrate
4.5 g total fat
42 mg cholesterol
315 mg sodium
1.7 g dietary fiber
15% calories from fat

Caloric Density: 312

Place salmon fillet in a large skillet. Combine the chopped vegetables and parsley and add to skillet with the fish. Combine the broth, white wine, soy sauce, and white wine Worcestershire sauce. Pour over the fish and vegetables. Bring to a simmer over medium heat. Reduce heat to low and cook, covered, about 8 minutes, or until the fish is cooked through. Carefully lift the salmon out of the skillet and set aside to cool. Strain the vegetables from the poaching liquid and allow them to cool. The poaching liquid can be discarded, or it can be strained, cooled, and frozen for use as a fish stock in another recipe.

In a medium bowl, combine the yogurt, dill, mustard, and tarragon with a whisk. Stir the cooled vegetables into the sauce.

Cut the salmon fillet into 4 pieces. Place each piece on a plate and drizzle with the sauce. Serve with boiled, baby red potatoes and steamed vegetables.

PORK FRIED RICE

MAKES 4 1½-CUP SERVINGS

2 cups cooked brown rice
vegetable oil cooking spray
1 Tbs. minced garlic
1 cup sliced green onion
1 cup thin sliced carrots
1 cup frozen thawed spinach, drained
6 ounces pork tenderloin, cut into small chunks
½ cup egg whites
1 cup nonfat, low-sodium chicken broth
2 Tbs. lite soy sauce
1 Tbs. natural rice wine vinegar
1 tsp. sesame oil
pinch of cayenne
pinch of ground ginger

NUTRITION
INFORMATION

Each serving contains
approximately:
239 calories
19 g protein
30 g carbohydrate
4.5 g total fat
23 mg cholesterol
168 mg sodium
4.5 g dietary fiber
17% calories from fat

Caloric Density: 318

Cook the brown rice according to package directions. For 2 cups of cooked brown rice you will need ¾ cup of uncooked brown rice and 1½ cups of water.

Generously spray a nonstick skillet with vegetable oil cooking spray and heat over medium-high heat. Sauté the garlic until golden, about 1 minute. Add the onion, carrots, and spinach and cook briefly, about 2 minutes. Add the pork loin and sauté for 2 minutes. Add the egg whites and scramble, then add the chicken broth, soy sauce, vinegar, sesame oil, cayenne, and ginger. Cook until the pork is done, about 5 minutes. Add the rice and stir well. Serve hot.

SPANISH-STYLE OMELET

MAKES 4 1-CUP SERVINGS

olive oil cooking spray
1/2 cup chopped onion
2 cloves garlic, minced
2 medium baking potatoes,
    washed and diced small
1 green pepper, diced
1 ripe tomato, diced
1 tsp. dried oregano
1 tsp. dried rosemary, chopped
ground black pepper, to taste
1 1/2 cups nonfat egg substitute

NUTRITION
INFORMATION

Each serving contains
approximately:
130 calories
13 g protein
18 g carbohydrate
0.5 g total fat
0 mg cholesterol
171 mg sodium
3 g dietary fiber
3% calories from fat

Caloric Density: 226

Generously spray a large nonstick skillet with olive oil cooking spray and heat over medium-high heat. Sauté the onion and garlic until golden, about 2 minutes. Add the potatoes, green pepper, tomato, and seasonings. Cook until tender, stirring frequently, about 5 to 6 minutes. Transfer potato mixture to a plate.

Clean and dry the skillet. Spray again with olive oil cooking spray and place over medium-high heat. Allow the pan to get hot, then pour the egg substitute into the pan. Using a rubber spatula, fold the egg from the outside into the center until the eggs are almost set. Add the potato mixture on top; allow all to heat through, keeping the omelet loose from the pan with the spatula. Remove from the stove. Cut into quarters and serve.

TURKEY LOAF WITH MUSHROOM SAUCE

MAKES 10 SERVINGS (with 2 Tbs. sauce)

vegetable oil cooking spray
1 cup chopped onion
1 cup chopped celery
1 Tbs. minced garlic
1/4 cup nonfat, low-sodium chicken broth
1 cup cooked brown rice
3 egg whites
1 6-ounce can tomato paste
1 tsp. dried thyme
1 tsp. dried oregano
ground black pepper, to taste
1/2 tsp. garlic powder
1 Tbs. red wine vinegar
1 1/4 pounds ground skinless turkey breast
2 Tbs. ketchup

NUTRITION
INFORMATION

Each serving contains
approximately:
172 calories
21 g protein
16 g carbohydrate
2 g total fat
41 mg cholesterol
176 mg sodium
2.3 g dietary fiber
11% calories from fat

Caloric Density: 332

Preheat oven to 350°. Lightly spray a 9 by 5-inch loaf pan with vegetable oil cooking spray. Generously spray a nonstick skillet with the cooking spray and heat over medium-high heat. Sauté the onion, celery, and garlic until golden brown and crisp-tender, about 3 minutes. Add the chicken broth and cook until it evaporates. Pour the onion mixture into a food processor and purée with the brown rice, egg whites, tomato paste, seasonings, and vinegar.

Place the puréed ingredients together with the ground turkey in a large mixing bowl and mix well. Place meatloaf in loaf pan and pat the top smooth. Glaze the top with the ketchup and put in the oven. Bake until done in the center, approximately 50 minutes. Allow to sit for a few minutes before removing from the pan. Slice and serve with the mushroom sauce.

Mushroom Sauce:
vegetable oil cooking spray
8 ounces sliced fresh mushrooms
1 cup nonfat, low-sodium chicken broth

1 Tbs. cornstarch
1 Tbs. balsamic vinegar
1 tsp. Worcestershire sauce
ground black pepper, to taste

Generously spray a large nonstick skillet with vegetable oil cooking spray and heat over medium-high heat. Saute the mushrooms until golden, about 3 or 4 minutes. Mix the chicken broth with the cornstarch, balsamic vinegar and Worcestershire and pour into the skillet, stirring constantly. Bring the mixture to a boil and season with black pepper. Simmer briefly and serve hot.

BANANA-BLUEBERRY RIPPLE "ICE CREAM"

MAKES 6 ½-CUP SERVINGS

3 medium bananas, peeled, wrapped in plastic
    and frozen until firm
½ cup nonfat milk or soy milk
1 16-ounce bag frozen blueberries

NUTRITION
INFORMATION

Each serving contains
approximately:
96 calories
1 g protein
23 g carbohydrate
less than 1 g total fat
0 mg cholesterol
6 mg sodium
4 g dietary fiber
7% calories from fat

Caloric Density: 301

Cut the frozen bananas into several pieces. Put the frozen banana pieces into a processor fitted with the steel chopping blade and process until smooth (add ¼ cup of the milk, if necessary, to facilitate processing). Transfer the frozen banana purée to a bowl and place in the freezer while you process the blueberries, but don't leave it in the freezer long enough to harden.

Wipe out the processor, add the frozen blueberries and process until smooth adding the remaining milk, if needed. Add the blueberries to the bowl with the bananas. Using a large fork, swirl the blueberry and banana purées together to make a ripple. Do not overmix. Spoon into 6 sundae dishes and serve while still frozen.

Do-Ahead Note: The "ice cream" may be made ahead and frozen. Cover it with plastic wrap and press down so that the plastic is touching the fruit. This will prevent it from icing over. Remove from the freezer to allow the "ice cream" to soften before serving.

FRESH STRAWBERRIES WITH STRAWBERRY-TOFU CUSTARD

MAKES 6 SERVINGS
(½ cup fruit, ½ cup sauce)

1 16-ounce bag frozen strawberries
1 12¼-ounce package lite "Silken" tofu
artificial sweetener, to taste
1 box (1 pint) fresh strawberries, washed and sliced

NUTRITION
INFORMATION

Each serving contains
approximately:
72 calories
5 g protein
12 g carbohydrate
1 g total fat
0 mg cholesterol
57 mg sodium
3.2 g dietary fiber
13% calories from fat

Caloric Density: 159

Defrost the frozen strawberries completely. Drain in a strainer set over a bowl and gently squeeze to remove as much liquid as possible.

Cream the tofu in a processor, fitted with the steel chopping blade. Add the drained, defrosted strawberries and purée until the mixture has the consistency of a smooth custard. Taste for sweetness and, if desired, add an artificial sweetener such as Equal, to taste. Place in the refrigerator to chill.

Divide the fresh, sliced strawberries into 6 dessert dishes, saving a few slices for garnishing.

Pour the custard over the strawberries and garnish with strawberry slices.

MOCHA CREAM WITH FRESH RASPBERRIES

MAKES 4 SERVINGS

NUTRITION
INFORMATION

1 box (1 pint) fresh raspberries
5 ounces extra firm "Silken" tofu
2 Tbs. prune purée (baby food)
3 Tbs. Dutch-process cocoa powder*
3 Tbs. mild molasses (such as Grandma's brand)
1 Tbs. powdered instant coffee, or coffee substitute
1 tsp. confectioners' sugar (optional)

Each serving contains
approximately:
102 calories
3 g protein
21 g carbohydrate
1.3 g total fat
0 mg cholesterol
32 mg sodium
3.7 g dietary fiber
11% calories from fat

Caloric Density: 431

Divide the fresh raspberries among 4 dessert dishes, saving a dozen or so for garnish.

Process the tofu in a processor until all large lumps have broken down. Add the remaining ingredients, except the optional confenctioners' sugar, and process until smooth and creamy. Transfer the mocha into a bowl and refrigerate until chilled.

Dust the garnish raspberries with confectioners' sugar, if desired. Spoon the chilled mocha cream over the raspberries in the dessert dishes and garnish with the sugared raspberries.

*Dutch-process cocoa is cocoa that has been processed with an alkali to reduce acidity. It has a much richer, more chocolate-like taste than regular cocoa. Regular cocoa would not be a good substitute. Dutch-process cocoa can be found in supermarkets and specialty food stores, or ask your store manager.

PEAR AND YOGURT PARFAIT

MAKES 4 1-CUP SERVINGS

4 ripe pears, peeled, cored, and diced
(Bosc, Bartlette or Anjou are best)
1 Tbs. fresh orange juice
½ tsp. ground cinnamon
dash of grated nutmeg
12 ounces light, nonfat vanilla yogurt
4 Tbs. Hershey's Lite Chocolate Syrup

NUTRITION
INFORMATION

Each serving contains
approximately:
158 calories
4 g protein
35 g carbohydrate
1 g total fat
0 mg cholesterol
55 mg sodium
4 g dietary fiber
6% calories from fat

Caloric Density: 289

Place diced pears, orange juice, cinnamon, and nutmeg in a microwave-safe container and stir well. Microwave until tender, about 12 minutes; stir half way through. Chill pears briefly in the refrigerator.

Place ⅓ cup yogurt in the bottom of 4 dessert glasses. Top with cooked pears then 1 tablespoon of Hershey's Lite Chocolate Syrup. Serve immediately or chill until ready to serve.

SPICED APPLE CRISP

MAKES 4 ½-CUP SERVINGS

5 red Delicious or Fuji apples,
    peeled, cored, and cut into wedges
1 Tbs. water
2 tsp. cornstarch
1 tsp. apple-pie spice
juice of ½ lemon (1 Tbs.)

Topping:
¼ cup crushed shredded wheat
pinch of ground cinnamon

NUTRITION INFORMATION

Each serving contains approximately:
116 calories
0.5 g protein
29 g carbohydrate
0.5 g total fat
0 mg cholesterol
less than 1 mg sodium
5 g dietary fiber
5% calories from fat

Caloric Density: 280

Combine apples, water, cornstarch, spice, and lemon juice in a medium mixing bowl. Mix well and place into a microwaveable container. Microwave on high for 10 minutes, or until apples are soft and juice is thick and clear. Divide among 4 dessert bowls. Top each serving with 1 tablespoon crushed shredded wheat and a sprinkle of cinnamon.

INDEX

PRITIKIN® CONTACT INFORMATION

For further information about the Pritikin® Lifestyle Support System, contact:

The World Wide Web: www.pritikin.com

The Longevity Centers: 1-800-421-9911, CA
                                             1-800-327-4914, FL

Personal Nutrition Assessment
and Lifestyle Coaching,
or Pritikin® Vitamins and Supplements: 1-800-658-2702

Home Exercise Equipment by Life Fitness®:   1-800-877-3867

Pritikin® Food Products   1-800-238-8090